Building the
Team from the
INSIDE ⇔ OUT

D1379531

Building the Team from the INSIDE ⬌ OUT

A Multi-Dimensional View of Leadership

Maryann Roefaro

A Waterside Publication

Published by Waterside Publications
ISBN: 978-1-937503-73-4
WPP125P

Manufactured in the United States of America or in Great Britain, when purchased outside of North or South America

Produced and distributed for
Waterside Publications by
Worthy Shorts Publisher Services BackOffice
A CustomWorthy edition

For further information contact
info@worthyshorts.com

I met Phyllis Price in the fall of 2011, after she left me a voice message requesting to meet. She wanted to know how "we did it."

"As a frequent visitor to Hematology-Oncology Associates, within a very large organization I observed a calm efficiency that was unsurpassed, while staff was catering daily to a seriously ill population. Staff at the facility was organized, attentive, supportive and seemingly unscathed by the pressure and problem solving challenges they faced each day in this world of illness and healing. Curious to know the secret of how an organization of this size, operated with such efficiency and what the recipe was to have employees so pleasantly and supportively interface with the clients served, the answer I received several times over was, Maryann Roefaro, our CEO. Several told me about monthly staff meetings, where Maryann utilizes an uplifting and inspiring talk, enjoyed by all and focused on a thought provoking keyword, or theme called an "8 ½ x 11." The employees told me that each talk is designed to bring out the personal best of each individual in the organization, and in doing so, the creation of a safe, caring, and high-achieving environment for the client. When professionals are encouraged to be their personal best in a safe and non-judgmental way, they can then become the caring, respectful, and responsible human beings they are meant to be. If the outgrowth of the lessons from Ms. Roefaro's leadership is an efficient, effective and compassionate organization, then we would all benefit from its message!"

Phyllis Price, Principal,
Casey Park Elementary School
Auburn, New York

Dedication

I dedicate this book, with all my love, to the one man who has been by my side, supporting all my endeavors and loving me unconditionally, all my life. The man who taught me to kill people with kindness, to understand that you catch more flies with honey than with vinegar, to put love into everything I do, and to jump every hurdle using every gift I possess. I lovingly and gratefully dedicate this book to my father, Renato J. Roefaro, Sr.

Acknowledgements

It is with incredible love and gratitude that I thank my family, friends and colleagues. To my immediate family, in order of appearance: I thank my mother and father, Angela Marie Roefaro and Renato J. Roefaro, Sr. Although I only had my mother on this earth for a short time, I would rather have had her for 14 years than spend 100 with anyone else. She was the first person in my life who helped me understand who I was and in her own special way, she was my first self-mastery mentor. She introduced me to a Divine Network of resources that she knew would illuminate my steps, all the days of my life. I thank my father for his unwavering love and support throughout my lifetime. His example laid the foundation for any success I have achieved. I thank my Grandmother, Leah Mirante Roefaro. With her unconditional love and untiring spirit, she taught me how to be resilient and strong, characteristics that came naturally to her. She made me believe that I could do anything! I thank my two brothers, Louis Roefaro and Renato Roefaro, Jr. They have taught me more than they will ever know and I love them with all my heart for the example they set for me and for their continual support and encouragement. I thank my step-mom, Carol Roefaro for her undying love and support. Her belief in me has been a great source of motivation in my life. There are no words to express my love and gratitude to my two daughters, Casey Angela Franz and Angela Marie Franz. They have brought me more joy than I ever imagined possible. They always provided the love, support, encouragement and pride that allowed me to be a successful working mother. With all my heart, I thank my husband, Tom Carranti. You have touched my heart and soul like none other. I love you for so many reasons and your support of my endeavors and help with this book has meant the world to me. To my step sons, Pio Carranti and Joseph Carranti, I'm forever grateful for your love and respect.

To my mentors, friends and colleagues, words can never adequately express my gratitude for what you have taught me, the extent to which you have supported me, and the level of dedication and hard work that so many of you have put forth to make me look good. There are so many, I can't thank you by name, but I hope you know that I carry much love and gratitude in my heart for you.

I would like to thank Dr. Paul Granato. He has been a mentor and friend for almost 30 years. It was his belief in me and his selfless sharing of knowledge and wisdom that jump started my career. I thank Dr. A. John Merola whose incredible passion for life, medicine, success and entrepreneurialism often provided the impetus for my personal and professional growth during the formative years of my career. I will always hold a special place in my heart for you and I'm so grateful for the plethora of opportunities you sent my way. I thank Drs. John J. Gullo, Anthony J. Scalzo, Jeffrey J. Kirshner, and Santo M. DiFino for starting a medical practice over 30 years ago that has developed into one of the cherished jewels of Central New York and for giving me the opportunity of a life-time. Dr. Gullo—I love you and it's been an incredible gift to spend most Monday mornings sharing and strategizing with you! I'm grateful to all the physicians at Hematology-Oncology Associates, especially those physicians who are my kindred spirits.

I would like to thank Dale H. Franz, my former husband and father of my children. Without your friendship, love and support for many years, I would never have been able to maintain balance in my life and achieve the success that I enjoyed. A special thank you to Elizabeth Williams for being a soul sister and imparting incredible spiritual wisdom to my life. I would like to thank Mary Schechter, Founder and President of the Intuitive Organization. You have become my partner in spirit to help transform workplaces from the inside-out. I would like to thank Bruce Wood, Esq. for the many years of his friendship and the expertise he has graciously shared with me. Bruce, you will never realize your contribution to my life and career—thanks so much! I would like to thank Gail Cowley for being a kindred spirit and a dear and trusted friend and advisor. I am forever grateful to Paul Cowley for his creative genius in designing the cover of this book! Thanks Gail and Paul and all the staff at Cowley and Associates.

I would like to thank all the leaders who ever worked with me, especially Corinne Ferrante and Janet Ricciardiello—what would I have ever done without you! You know how much you mean to me and I can't thank you enough for the years by my side!

Hematology-Oncology Associates of CNY continues to be one of the greatest gifts to my life and career. It is with heartfelt love and appreciation that I thank my "Kitchen Table"/ Senior Leadership Team: Mary Stone, Kelly Vaccaro, Michael Cretaro, Kim DeRosa Fish, Kim Roddy, Jonas Congelli, Marsha DeVita and Maria Grice. Individually and together, we continue to traverse the self-mastery journey. We have accomplished a great deal and I am truly blessed to work so closely with some of the finest leaders I have known. Our team and our organization is strong and successful because of the sum of our parts! A special thank you to my dear friend and colleague, Gussie Sorensen. You have selflessly shared your experience and wisdom into the human psyche with me for almost 10 years and I am forever grateful.

I would like to thank the entire staff at Hematology-Oncology Associates of CNY. Our journey together has taught me much about the mastery of self, the real meaning of success and the tapestry of love that can be woven in the work place. It is a privilege to work with the finest. Thanks for listening to my 8 ½ x 11 snippets for almost 10 years!

I'd like to thank my agent, Bill Gladstone and the staff at Waterside Publications and Worthy Shorts, especially Gene Schwartz and Otto Barz.

Last but always first, I thank the Divine Infrastructure that illuminates my life, envelops me with unconditional love and co-creates the wonderful and challenging world of which we are one.

I am so filled with gratitude and love—thank you to everyone I mentioned and all those that hold a special place in my heart that have provided great love and support to my life.

Table of Contents

8 ½ x 11s

Building the Team from the Team from the INSIDE ⇔ OUT

Chapter One

Every relationship we have depends on the one we have with our self

Are you happy? Do you ever wonder why you react to life the way you do? Do the actions of others ever confuse or hurt you? Do you ever dread going to work because of the drama or stress that awaits you? Are you bothered by a world that can't live in peace and unity? Does the uncertainly of your world foster anxiety that alters your mood or disrupts your sleep? Do you look down the corridor of potential or limitation when you get out of bed in the morning? Each day, we are the *only* people responsible for how we view the world and the challenges that arise. We decide our own fate and the answers to all these questions and more are dependent upon how we view ourselves and life and *not* by what is happening around us. The decision to be happy and tolerant becomes easier when we understand who we are and recognize that things are not always what they appear to be. Whether you're a leader in an organization or a leader via the example by which you live your life or run your household, leadership is an incredibly important component of life.

Every relationship we have depends on the relationship we have with our self. Every member of a work team, irrespective of their position or level of responsibility in a company or family, thinks, believes and therefore functions from the perspectives that are related to the core beliefs they hold about themselves. Patterns of thought create our life. These patterns generate emotions all day, every day, whether at work or not. Some patterns are good for us and others are not. Sometimes living within these patterns becomes so routine and comfortable that even when they're not in our best interest, we still immerse ourselves in them and convince ourselves that nothing needs to change. We may get frustrated with ourselves, but not everybody has the energy or desire to look inside. Clearing the cob webs in our consciousness may be a frightening alternative. The thoughts that create our existence demonstrate equal opportunity in the work place, as well as at home or anyplace. A dysfunctional team or work group can't be fixed unless the people on the team are willing to take a look inside. A look at the triggers that send them into that whirl of dysfunction, as the team will only be as good as the sum of its parts.

This book will build an awareness of the relationship between the self and the effectiveness of leaders, teams and work groups—any kind of work group. It will be helpful to anyone in a supervisory, management or leadership position but it will also be helpful to those individuals who are not in traditional leadership positions but exemplify their leadership skills by the way they live their lives. It will provide a blue print of thought to enable and enrich organizational development by enhancing the self-realization of the individuals that make up the group. More simply said, this book has to potential to provide a wake-up call. A wake-up call for leaders and employees that will ultimately create a more successful and love filled work environment. It will provide a view of leadership that contains multiple dimensions in its panoramic outlook. It will precipitate the intimate scrutiny of personal priorities. This book will outline the benefits of self-realization as it relates to a happier and more fulfilled life and therefore a more harmonious, fulfilling and effective work environment. The chapters that follow can provide insights to enable the reader to clear the clutter that resides in their mind, body and spirit so they can remember who they really are—and recognize the power and innate gifts that reside within the self. I'm speaking of the power that resides within the layers of consciousness that conjure, create and implement the character and quality of our daily lives. I write this book with respect to all people, as I believe everyone is in the perfect place on their individual journey. I offer many concepts and philosophies that have worked for me and the teams of which I have had the privilege to lead for almost 30 years. Only the reader can validate their truth, as each path is different and in perfect order; perfect order because every situation offers growth of some kind. Perhaps the time to continue your journey with some new ideas or perspectives is now?

Some elements of this book may resonate within and some may not, but the exercises in thought may ultimately provide incredible benefits. This book introduces concepts that most leadership books would not include as they either fall outside most leaders' perimeter of awareness or would be viewed as concepts not appropriate for discussion or involvement in the work place. I believe this book offers a unique paradigm of leadership—a look at leadership from the inside-out where we build the aggregate by building the character and resilience of its parts, eliminating fear whenever possible. Eliminating fear and replacing it with love, starting with the love of self.

A paradigm shift is a pervasive change in thinking from accepted standards or accepted points of view to a new way. This new way can be precipitated by some new scientific discovery, invention or new information that provides a whole new way of thinking or doing things. We have options at our fingertips that didn't exist a month ago, let alone years ago. When a paradigm changes, the old adage states, everyone goes back to zero. What made a leader or company successful yesterday does not guarantee success tomorrow. When a significant change in thinking occurs or a belief system is appreciably altered and accepted by the masses, those who cannot embrace the new thought system or paradigm may find themselves relics. The successful leaders of tomorrow will not be among the relics. The very characteristics that made some leaders successful many years ago may inhibit their success today. Workers want to be empowered, nurtured in a climate of independence, and managed in a culture of respect and appreciation. Our younger adults have grown up in a world of technology with new words, flavors, and modes of communication. Good employees will be drawn to organizations that care about them and the world in which they live. Globally, people are getting tired of living in fear and so many are searching for meaning and sustenance in a confusing world.

You're reading this book for a reason. You may not agree with everything, but with an open mind, I hope you will be motivated to offer a change to your world by contemplating the style in which you think and perceive. This book is a guide to a journey within the self that will expand the understanding of self to create satisfaction and fulfillment in your life—including your work life. It will enrich interactions with others by assisting in the development of greater tolerance, a richer acknowledgement of human frailty and a contemplation of intention versus words heard and actions witnessed.

Corrupt systems that do not serve the good of the whole are breaking down and are no longer sustainable. The world is in tumultuous flux, as the hunger for freedom and the acknowledgment of humanity are moved to the front burners. At every turn, another company is going "green" and more individuals are refocusing attention on our beautiful and abundant planet, recognizing its years of abuse and neglect. The light that shines forth to heal the world has never been brighter and our population is becoming less tolerant of spiritual ignorance and pomposity. The potential for a world of peace is becoming aligned with the goals and objectives of a greater number of people. There is great courage and conviction seen among the people of the world. A leader understands this and subtly facilitates and supports this recognition to their constituents, irrespective of the group's size, type, location and mission because they understand the potential of humanity and how it all intertwines to create the whole. Just as the pebble in the water ripples far and wide, everything we say and do adds to the sum of the whole.

The day will come when the thoughts of the people or the collective consciousness of a work group or organization will be used to manifest success in ways that were previously unfathomable. The collective consciousness represents the sum total of the thoughts or shared beliefs of the people who make up the group that defines the collection. There can be the collective consciousness of a team or an organization, as well as communities, countries and the world. I believe there is energy associated with the collective thoughts of a group. I'm confident that this energy plays a greater role than most people could imagine. I'm not sure many people give credence or thought to this idea, but I think the energy has a huge impact on our lives. A leader of the future will know how to foster this consciousness for the good of the organization and for the good of the whole. With the support of others, it will be easier than anyone thought it could be and it will redefine the way people do business. Integrity will be the word of the day and hard work and dedication will flow freely from the people who love what they do because they are able to make a difference each day that they do it. Accountability will become an innate by-product of this leadership paradigm, as people will understand the level of responsibility that must be categorized to the self.

We currently live in a world where there is a lack of accountability and blame flows freely. The power that resides in each of us maintains the ability to change our life by changing our thoughts. Thoughts related to self that drive the feelings and emotions of our lives are not segregated into family, friends, home, work, etc. Many pretend and work very hard to be different people in different places but how we think makes us who we are—and who we are is who we are, irrespective of location.

When we journey the path of self-mastery, we transform into a more confident and happy human being because we clear the clutter that silently or overtly resides within the core of our being. Clutter that is comprised of the people, places, events and things we've held inside since childhood. The clutter that is the product of all the thoughts and experiences we've had in our lives; the clutter that resides in the sea of consciousness of which we may be aware or totally oblivious.

This transcendence and individual growth allows for the building of highly effective work teams, more stable and successful corporations and a more cohesive world trade. The greatest gift a leader can give their team is to provide an atmosphere where their key leaders, managers and staff can figure out who they are and believe that they were born with the tools they need to be successful. Before a leader can walk the talk, however, they have to believe it and understand it themselves. They need to have concepts like self-mastery baked into the being of who they are, so the flow of words and actions are natural. A leader that truly serves the people helps to build a consciousness of cooperation, quality and accountability. When any group of people working towards a common goal comes together with this individual knowing, the results can be astonishing.

Every leader struggles to build teams that are void of dysfunction. Key leadership personnel spend years in academic training and more years developing wisdom and expertise from experience. But in the end, the team will be as functional as the aggregate of its parts—the cumulative level of self-mastery and evolution of each individual. This phenomenon extends to the entire work force. A unified organization, melded together in love and spirit knows no boundaries for success. It's time for the kind of leaders so caught up in a corporate culture of fear to look within themselves to know, trust and explore who they are and what makes them act and react to the stimuli of life. Perhaps the word *spiritual* does not feel like it belongs in the work place but now is the time to change that leadership paradigm and work towards a love based leadership style instead of a fear based leadership style. Spirituality is at the core of who we are. It's the intangible part of ourselves that desires and feels a connection with the rest of the world and everything in it. It's the part of ourselves that seeks meaning and knows we have the ability to transform our lives. Spirituality is that part of us that yearns to give to others and make a significant contribution to our world. It's recognition that we are not alone and we have Divine resources to assist us on our journey. It's the ultimate recognition that everything is Divine. Perhaps you accept the hypothesis that we are spiritual beings having a physical experience? If so, you may agree that if we're going to figure out who we are and how we can be happy and successful, we can't ignore the option that we are a spirit whose essence has decided to temporarily live in the land of opportunity called earth. A land of opportunity through challenges and celebrations—through love and a lack thereof. Speaking about the mind-body-spirit connection is a popular concept, one that we will discuss in detail in this book. All those aspects, however, are not separate; they are intertwined and inseparable and make us whole. If our mind or body or spirit is wounded or out of alignment, it will affect our entire being. I hope that someday, people will truly begin to understand that we are all *one* and that we are interconnected and woven together in this tapestry called humanness. When that is acknowledged, we will understand that hurting one means hurting all. When these concepts are acknowledged, the paradigm shifts and everyone living in the old energy of leadership and/or corporate, political or social greed, goes back to "start here."

Chapter Two

The cascades of fear . . .

News spread fast and attorneys and consultants were like vultures circling their prey, waiting for the opportunity to pounce and feast upon the delectable, vulnerable and perishable personnel that would soon be classified as expendable assets. As soon as a management team hears, we're merging, consolidating, integrating or some other synonym for this joining in corporate matrimony, the thermometer of fear begins to rise faster than the mercury in a rectal thermometer placed into the anus of a baby with a 104 degree temperature!

The fantasizing commences, as the patterns of thought provoke emotions related to fear and anxiety. What will this mean for me? The subtle wheels of fight or flight begin to turn. Over time, through meetings and spreadsheets and analyses and proformas, stress permeates the core of many. The uncertainty erodes the defenses and impermeability to stress becomes challenged. At times the heart rate may increase as blood is shunted to the extremities to provide fuel for the run. Breathing may become more shallow and rapid at times, while the mind can't stop calculating the ratio of possibilities to the sum of mortgage payments, car leases, student loans, and other expenses of daily living. Epinephrine begins to be pumped out and the immune system takes a back burner to allow the endocrine and nervous systems to produce the chemicals and transmitters necessary to create a neuro-network of survival. If talks of this merger take a long time, the vulnerable may even find themselves with a new dis-ease.

Survival strategies begin to take place as the leaders on the team wiggle and weasel their way to safety. The good of the whole may or may not be ignored, as survival takes precedence. Will it be survival of the fittest and what will define the fittest? Will it be the person or people who can shove their heads so far up the boss' or consultant's butt that they can no longer see the light of day but will find themselves in a nice warm, safe spot when the pink slips are distributed? Will the fittest be the people who speak their truth and work for the good of the whole, putting their personal agendas aside? Will the fittest be the biggest bullshitters among the group who can talk the corporate line and ignore the mind, body and spirits of the truly greatest assets of the corporation—the employees? Ultimately the character of the fittest will render the sustainability of the organization—for the tone and personality of the new entity will give birth from the people at the top of the food chain, and the strength of the whole will be dependent upon the sum of its parts.

And at the end of the race, those left standing will begin to build the new work place. They will surely rejoice at their success but **will they** ponder the laws of the Universe and contemplate the karma they have created along the way? Will they look within themselves to understand the role they have played and contemplate the changes in the fabric of existence that have resulted from the thoughts, emotions and actions they created? Will they examine the quality and quantity of energy they expended and contemplate how that has affected and will continue to affect their state of health and well-being? Will they wonder how their intentions and actions have affected and will continue to affect others?

It was almost 15 years ago and I was one of the Corporate Vice Presidents of one of the largest acute care hospitals in our community. Every Tuesday I sat among the Senior Leadership group as plans to form an alliance with a community hospital were created. One day, the familiar voice within me spoke, as there were a couple of important facets to acknowledge. One of the most important was that each person at that big table were products of a unique and individual life with challenges and celebrations, grounded in love and fear that not only made them who they were but seasoned every opinion and perception they harbored and exemplified about themselves and everyone else. We all grow in rain and sunshine but the proportions of each are never known to another and for this reason, one must become the observer without judgment. It was important that I recognized that facet of exchange.

This group of well-intentioned humans was establishing new rules for the future. Not dissimilar from other groups of well-intentioned people, humans have been creating illusions of existence for mankind since the beginning of time. For millennia, groups of different sizes, colors and shapes have seeded the future with perhaps well-intentioned, yet dogmatic theories, policies, procedures and standard operating principles. Many people look around and believe everything they see is real. Ways of doing things and belief systems are handed down from generation to generation and are often accepted as correct and true without question. My father always taught me to believe half of what I saw and nothing of what I heard. That was great advice and I am going to take that one step further and say, try believing nothing of what you hear or see that has been created and sustained by the human ego, the need for power and/or control. Perhaps you can accept the *potential* that just about everything is an illusion created by mankind? These illusions have become so customary and familiar that most people would never stop to think that it is people who have created the world of which we live. This may be a rather difficult concept to grasp and more explanation into this blueprint of thought will be addressed later in this book—so hold on to those thoughts and questions. In the mean time, stop a moment and ask yourself what part of life cannot change? Perhaps it is only that which cannot change that is real?

The scenario of the merger or acquisition and its accompanied changes in emotions and behaviors described earlier in this chapter occurs in the work place whenever significant changes are on the horizon. Sometimes it takes place when non-significant changes of daily work-life occur. In some organizations, it takes place daily. An integration or merger is not necessary to precipitate fear within a leadership and work group. Fear develops whenever a person feels threatened by change or just plain threatened. That catalyst could be as benign as the addition of a new team member or as malignant as corruption and deceit. When any circumstance renders a person fearful that the potential to lose their status, income, or job security surfaces or instigates them to perceive that they are not good enough, liked enough, or trusted enough, the wheels of survival connected to a frame of irrational self-talk, peddled by fear, will kick in a cascade of emotions, feelings and actions. At some level this renders the employee or leader far more inefficient because there is a magnitude of energy expended in the wrong direction and they will merely attract that which they fear the most. When these perceptions are unfounded and are created by the fears and clutter that reside deeply within a person's consciousness, the workplace takes a financial and energetic hit. When the hours of drama and associated lost work time are multiplied by the compensation of an employee, one can estimate and calculate the financial burden fear and drama pose to an organization. This financial, energetic or productivity drain can be a common phenomenon at work and at home. By acknowledging and understanding the triggers, actions and reactions associated with the fear of not being good enough and falling short of the expectations people place upon themselves, the first steps in healing and eliminating such pollution from one's life takes place.

Fear is not in the best interest of anyone or any corporation. Although many are cognizant of this at a conscious level, it still becomes the most common and dominant facet in some people's lives and in organizations. Fear creates drama and many feed and need drama. Fear and drama are great attention grabbers. All one need to do is watch the news or read the newspaper to witness the birth and propagation of fear. There are people so familiar with the feelings of fear that living in fear has become unrecognizable and comfortable. Drama is all around us, bombarding our airways and individual space, like a vacuum whose job it is to suck people into the vat.

When a person functions from a survival perspective, fearing and working diligently not to get fired or to be liked by everyone, they become a liability to an organization. Some of the most highly functioning and best employees can nest inside this paradox of ineffectiveness from time to time. This occurrence could be rare, intermittent or continual. Very often, a person will not realize that their decisions, actions and orders come from a base of fear instead of love and confidence. Fear prevents organizations and people from taking risks. Risk is often a necessary and integral component of success. Over time, when enough of this behavior becomes rampant, an organization will become paralyzed. Ultimately this can result in the crumbling of an organization to extinction.

Times of uncertainty and change that precipitate concern and anxiety are unavoidable. The ability of a leader to analytically evaluate the potential and risk of any strategic initiative, coupled with an intuitive knowing of the likelihood of its success are invaluable. Invaluable but uncommon—as many leaders pay little attention to the development, enrichment or understanding of their level of intuitive skill. Intuition is information received within that instills a *knowing* of some circumstance or event. It is information or a feeling that may or may not be consistent with human logic. Intuition is from a part of ourselves that can access knowledge and wisdom from a divine source that resides in every person. The more a person becomes aware of this innate gift, the more they will acknowledge the communication and insights that are intuitive in nature. The more a person acknowledges these insights the more they will begin to trust them. The more we trust our intuition, the easier it is to shift our awareness to that additional source of knowledge and wisdom. Some may think there is no use for intuition in the work place. I however, in my over 25 years of leadership, find it essential.

A leader, while keeping their mind, body and spirit on the mission, deals with anxiety before it can fester and render an employee or work group dysfunctional. A leader should be proactive and understand the human condition and concepts of consciousness. If they're really good, they can squelch drama before it starts. Many people think this is immensely difficult. It is not. It does require a fair amount of energy and a sincere desire, however. Sincerity that permeates every fiber of one's being and allows a person to evolve to greater levels of knowing and loving themselves, thereby becoming more confident and resilient. It requires sincerity that allows one to see past the words and actions of people and understand that intention is what matters and there is a reason for life's patterns. Loving and understanding the human condition of another person or work group is an essential element of good leadership but to do so, one must first love and understand themselves. A person must be able to recognize the presence of fear and replace it with love. This knowing and loving of self, will allow any person to become a better listener, friend, parent, partner, worker or leader. This type of leader has great confidence and self-control, as they have learned how to assess and control their mental and emotional bodies. Some may have worked on this at a cognitive level and others may have worked on these facets of consciousness without being aware—perhaps those born to lead. Even those people who are not born leaders can provide good, solid leadership if they evolve to understand themselves and others with a level of tolerance, understanding, commitment and self-mastery.

The two fundamental, core emotions of which all other emotions are born are love and fear—the myriad of others are extensions of these two core emotions. If there are only two basic emotions, then leadership can either be fear based or love based. The paradigm of leadership I hope to foster from this book is love and intuitive based leadership. Make no mistake, however, in thinking that love based leadership is touchy feely and discards accountability, hard work, efficiency and excellence. Loved based leadership means that people are expected to do the work from the inside-out, working to understand why they think and act the way they do, how it affects others, how others affect them and how it all affects the team and organization. Love based leadership is the type of leadership that promotes self-directed, excellence seeking work teams and empowered employees. Love based leadership is fair and consistent and continually works towards the good of the whole. Love based leadership provides clear expectations and all the tools necessary to get the job done efficiently with the right people, working to eliminate drama and mediocrity. Love based leadership provides continual feedback of performance and re-directs those who are not right for the team to move into their next learning opportunity. Love based leadership supports high profits and a reinvestment of resources for the people. Love based leadership is encouraged and accelerated through self-mastery because every relationship we have depends on the one we have with our self. An organization whose culture fosters love based leadership and decision making is an honest, communicative place to work where people are kind to one another and where success is shared and celebrated by everyone. It's the organization in which people wake up in the morning and like to go to work. It's the kind of organization that helps to see and bring out the best in people. It's the kind of organization that lets the employees know they matter. It's the kind of organization that treats all people with respect and dignity. It's the kind of organization that will not accept mediocrity, the victim mentality and terminates those people who do not live the philosophies, values and mission of the organization. It's the kind of organization that will not tolerate bullies. It's the kind of organization that has a great reputation and receives resumes every day.

Thoughts created by the human mind are frequencies that love, heal, enrich, neglect or pollute our environment. Our thoughts are the creators and destroyers of our levels of happiness, contentment and success in life. They are the building blocks of the life we create at home, at work and at play. We readily accept that the world is filled with frequencies that we can't see. A Blackberry or iPhone responds to a multitude of frequencies that most people do not contemplate. People just take advantage of these frequencies through phone, scheduling, email, tasks, notes and internet access that is in complete harmony with the computers that serve this exchange in "real" time. It is foolish to think that the thoughts of mankind are not frequencies that affect our world, as well. A leader must know and understand how these frequencies "sync" to create the organizations they lead.

Chapter Three

The Real Power . . . working from the inside-out

Leonardo da Vinci said, "One can have no smaller or greater mastery than mastery of oneself." As with all people, the power that every leader is looking for can only be found within themselves. One of the most significant misunderstandings that I have witnessed in my career is the belief that power comes from force—albeit often subtle and inconspicuous –placed upon those in a subordinate role to the leader. Self mastery is the never-ending journey towards understanding who we are and how we are connected to everyone and everything. It is not an event or destination, yet a continual journey of the evolution of the mind, body and spirit. It is an understanding at the deepest level of our being that we are the writers, directors and producers of our lifetimes. The greatest power we have is the one that resides within ourselves. The greatest leaders will provide an environment that creates, fosters and maintains a consciousness where every employee can derive that conclusion, on their own, to build an organization where anything that is possible, becomes possible.

A leader is not inflated by the suppression of others. Only a weasel, disguised as a leader, can be pumped up by the sucking sounds of the people who do the work. A leader is there to serve. Each day, a leader should ask themselves what they will do to make it a better place for people to work—how they will facilitate resolutions to global issues—how they will remove the barriers that keep people from being fulfilled and productive—and how they will make a significant contribution to the longevity and prosperity of the whole. There are many wonderful benefits when one is in a position of leadership and with these benefits comes great responsibility. There is no need to sound the leadership trumpets and ensure people understand your arrival in this role—for a great leader rarely focuses on the position or title they hold but on their ability to effectuate change through their potential to access information, goods and services. They focus on establishing relationships with people. The title allows for great opportunity but the title is just a title. People inflated by their titles need to get over themselves and realize that a title is a blessing and an opportunity to be used for the good of the whole. When people get together to accomplish any goal, attitude, knowledge, wisdom, skills, teamwork and the ability to gain access to what is needed are paramount. Effective leaders and smart people need not herald their level of skill and intelligence to the world, the world will know it. The same goes for titles—when you're good, people will know who you are and the contribution you make to an organization.

When speaking about power and positions, anyone who has ever worked for a micromanager has an intimate understanding of its definition and the characteristics that make up this type of manager. A true leader will not work for a micromanager for they will not allow any individual to snuff the flame of their creativity and independence from their midst. A micromanager is in need of enriching their self-mastery journey because it is fear and insecurity that drives that leadership style. It's difficult to trust other people when a person can't trust themselves. Micromanagement is exhausting for subordinates and their workgroups. Long term, micromanagers will be ineffective and the workgroup will be far less successful than the potential that may have originally existed. It is highly likely that fear will have permeated more than the personality of the work team as its tentacles often stifle creativity and illicit bouts of decision making paralysis throughout. Micromanagers don't like to take many risks, as the fear that permeates their thoughts (conscious and otherwise) affects the decisions they make. It's better to swing and strike out sometimes, then to never swing at all. The potential to hit a home run will never be met if the fear of striking out takes precedence and prevents the swing in the first place. Some micromanagers don't realize that they are one. That mystery is easily solved for those leaders who wonder and want to know. They would merely have to ask somebody who reported to them that was brave enough to have the verbal exchange. It's essential that this subordinate, however, was made to feel safe about having the discussion. They would need to feel confident that negative consequences would not follow an honest dialog.

Harmony in the work place is essential for people to want to come to work. If somebody dreads their workday, their attitudes and productivity will reflect such. If an organization expects an individual to put their work before their family or quality of life, the organization will ultimately lose, as the qualities that make a person a true asset include balance, self-love and self-respect. An organization will never be an employer of choice without harmony, good morale and enough money to get the job done correctly and enough profits to reinvest in the people and structure.

There are too many people holding others responsible for their happiness and success. There are too many people making excuses, playing the blame game and trying to change and control other people. There are too many managers placing expectations on their staff without communicating effectively or working from a position of fear instead of love. There is no place for a victim in a successful organization and a culture that creates or fosters a victim mentality will be fueled by mediocrity.

Understanding the power of our thoughts can elucidate the power and mystery that resides within oneself. The hallmark of thoughts is not only the cascade of effects they have on our body, but their ability to create the collective consciousness of which we exist. In our physical state of being, our thoughts form the energy that permeates our earthly existence and creates the circumstances of our life on earth. Thoughts are things and are a form of energy and matter. As previously stated, the sum total of the thoughts, energy and associated vibration that is exuded by each one of us, often referred to as the collective consciousness, is the energy or vibration that individually and cumulatively makes up the world in which we live. This energy, representative of the thoughts of humankind that can choose to think freely, forms the building blocks of the truth and illusions that surround us in our daily lives. The interconnectedness of each of us is undeniable and when one begins to contemplate the synchronicities of our existence, the divine nature of each of us begins to shine through.

Although it is not appropriate for religion or religious beliefs to become a part of the workplace, there are non-controversial, love related spiritual parameters that should be recognized and nurtured to traverse the management terrain of the coming decades. This all begins with the love of self because everything we think and do stems from our level of self-love.

How often have you met someone who you liked instantaneously and felt like you've known them for years? How often have you met somebody and sensed their negativity and knew immediately that their personality or energy was incompatible with your own? Have you ever said, "I just didn't get a good vibe from him/her?" Have you ever said, "I really like him/her but there was no chemistry between us?" Have you ever walked into a room and sensed the emotion of joy or anger? Have you ever said, "The tension was so great you could cut it with a knife?" Have you ever known that somebody entered a room but you didn't see them, you felt them? Have you ever thought of somebody and the phone rings shortly after? These are only a few of the daily examples that allow us to recognize forces that are unseen but impact our lives. We are connected at levels that fall outside our human capacity to understand.

There are synchronicities all around us and if we pay attention, miracles occur on a daily basis. How does a teacher know that the student has learned? Can they see learning? Can they put their hands on proof that the words and symbols were assimilated into the mind of the student? No. The teacher, however, can witness or experience the knowledge as it changes form and is exemplified by actions. Life is filled with examples of things that cannot be explained by the five senses but are there to serve as a question mark. They spark thought and provide glimpses of what can't be seen but can be known and felt by the heart.

Self mastery leads to a knowing that we are all of the light, a light that shines in each of us with a brilliance reflected by our capacity to love and be loved. This degree of brilliance is a representation of the magnitude of love and gratitude that permeates our thoughts, our actions and our being. The capacity to love and be grateful is equally available to everyone. The light that shines within each of us is the innate, Creator given gift of unconditional love potential. Our divinity is this light that shines forth to illuminate our world. It is this light that illuminates the recognition of souls—it allows us to know one another at a level of consciousness of which we may be unaware.

There are many reasons why we work at the places we do with the people we encounter. If you take a moment to think about it, most all of us spend the majority of our time with people who don't mean the very most to us. We are hired to do a job and jobs come in all kinds of shapes, sizes and varieties. From a spiritual standpoint, the people we have chosen to work with provide us with opportunities for growth. Our biggest irritants will provide the greatest potential for our growth for they will be the mirrors that reflect the parts of ourselves that we desire to least explore. In our careers or in the workplace, as with life in general, there are no failures, but many redirections. There are no failures because there is a reason for everything and everything that happens is for our highest good and is orchestrated (in one way or another) by ourselves.

One objective in life that carries over into the work place is understanding the role our egos play in our lives. An important exercise is allowing our higher-self to create and control our existence instead of allowing our egos. For ease of understanding, let us divide ourselves into two fundamental parts. Let's say that one part of us is our spirit and the other part is our ego. Spirit is the dealer of love and ego is the dealer of fear. Some refer to our spirit as our intuitive self, our higher self, our divine self, our God self or perhaps our superconscious mind. For many leaders, their ego is on autopilot and every decision they make is derived from the very dense, human part of themselves that acts and reacts from a position of fear. It is not easy to always recognize the many faces of fear. Egos run rampant in the work place, as many are oblivious to the assistance our spirit can provide and don't realize the position that fear occupies in their life and decision making. Some resist the knowing of their higher self and inadvertently make a decision every day to function from a position of fear or density, because it is more comfortable and familiar. For these people, the familiarity of anger, resentment, judgment, prejudice, or negativity is comfortable. Metaphysically, these are dense thoughts and states of being. What does that mean? The less "light" a thought, emotion or feeling possesses the more dense it is. The more "light" a thought, emotion or feeling possesses, the less dense it is. Love equals light, fear and all the manifestations thereof equal density. So, the more love, the more light the less dense. The more fear, the less light the more dense. The higher self is that part of ourselves that is love and light. It is divine and holds all the truths and wisdom of ourselves and the world. I think there is a misunderstanding of the word enlightened. Enlightenment is not exclusive to the gurus, avatars, saints and the holy of holies. The people who walk this earth in a state of enlightenment have simply remembered their divinity and understand that every tool they need to be happy and successful can be found within. Enlightenment is knowing and feeling the connection to everyone and everything. It's walking each day in the "oneness" and it's not outside our grasp. The more we allow our spirit, our higher self, to dictate our decisions, the less of a role our ego plays in our lives. The less our ego operates our thoughts and actions of daily living, the higher our potential for contentment and success. Our ego is the producer, processor and distributor of earthly limitations. Our ego is the manifestor of fear and the creator of the self-talk that runs rampant throughout our days, sabotaging our self-love, self-discipline, self-confidence and our self-reliant sustainability.

Our higher self is the producer, processor and distributor of potential. A life driven by spirit directed intentions yields a path of blissful ease in a complex world. A life driven by spirit renders thoughts that are born within the oneness of life. In addition, these thoughts elicit energy that fosters chemical reactions in the body representative of health and wellness. When the spirit reigns, life is good. Life is really, really good.

We all have what I term a "baseline titer of happiness." This baseline titer represents our core level of happiness and it will be addressed in greater deal in Chapter Seven, but I'd like to mention something about it here. There are people who are generally happy and those who are generally not happy. When a happy person with a high base line titer of happiness experiences life's challenges that sadden or upset them, the level of happiness they exude during this time may drop below their baseline, but in time, it returns to their usual core status because they are innately happy people. It resumes primarily because the person views every challenge as an opportunity for growth and accepts those challenges as a loving part of life. They understand that the greatest self growth comes from times of adversity or challenge. As my mother used to say, "For every pain that we must bear, every sorrow, every care, there is a reason" (I'm sure that was a poem that she did not write—sorry I can't give credit to whom it's due—but for me, the credit goes to her). When a person perceives that things are extraordinarily great, their baseline titer of happiness may extend above their core level or baseline, but in time, as normality resumes, their level of happiness returns to its usual status. People often wish for something—a new job, a new house, more money, a child, a spouse—thinking that that will finally make them happy, only to realize, in time, they're back where they started. The only way to increase a baseline titer of happiness is through self-love, self-discovery and self-mastery. We can build that self-love and enrich our spirituality through immersion. This will be discussed more in later chapters, but by immersing ourselves in love based decision making, immersing ourselves in opportunities to forgive, immersing ourselves in feelings of gratitude and appreciation, and immersing ourselves in service to others, our spirituality and self-love deepens and we begin to feel palpable changes within ourselves that cannot be described or attributed to human, linear language.

Mastery of self is a journey that occurs on many levels of consciousness. It is a journey and a process by which our humanness becomes less ego and more spirit. It's arriving at a place in our self-realization journey when we can immediately assess the influence our ego is having on our mind, body and actions because we're so aware of what life is like when our thoughts, emotions, and feelings are generated by our egoic nature. Mastery is when love and gratitude are the fundamental elements that drive our thoughts, feelings and emotions. It is an elucidation of the truth and a realization of the magnitude of illusions that crowd our everyday lives. This journey allows us to find our authenticity—our preciousness—the gift our life provides to the world. This authenticity of really knowing and understanding ourselves provides a more loving environment for our thoughts, perceptions and actions. In that environment of love, most things look and feel better.

Self-mastery is achieved when a person has no needs but abundance fills their existence. This lack of need has nothing to do with material possessions. Abandoning personal wealth or living in a state of poverty are not prerequisites for this state of mastery. It's about waking up to what is important in life and the true necessity to love oneself and have the best relationship with the self that is possible. A relationship that is based on honesty and an integration of positive thought processes such that living a positive life becomes a habit and anything else feels wrong. Self-love becomes so natural that a person no longer has to think about maintaining a positive attitude and counting their blessings instead of their problems, as it becomes a natural and effortless aspect of living. This positive embrace is a natural state of being when one has journeyed the path to self-mastery successfully.

Self-mastery is not about how much one has, but it is about how much one gives. It's not about the magnitude of wealth and possessions one holds, it's about not being attached to them for happiness but enjoying them as gifts of this lifetime. It's about developing, working for and cherishing preferences, but not making these material possessions rule our existence and dictate our lives. It's not about penalizing the self by limiting that which makes us happy from a material perspective, it's about being grateful, sharing and giving with and through the indices of love. No matter how smart or wise we are, it's essential to recognize that information and wisdom exists outside our sphere of knowledge. We should always be open minded to new information, messages and revelations. It's imperative to maintain an open mind without allowing our ego or the man made dogmas of control and limitation to establish the framework for our faith, beliefs and spirituality. One should maintain a constant willingness to accept new revelations that occur from the inside-out. We must be open-minded and humble enough to accept that our previous hypotheses and paradigms may be flawed or incomplete. As with new scientific discoveries that replace old schools of thought, when our minds are open to a spirit driven life, the observations and empirical data may show that man-made dogmas and beliefs provided a fine foundation but the time has come for new revelations to be accepted and integrated. The best revelations are those elucidated by the divinity within ourselves; information and feelings we gather from time alone, in the stillness, that resonate to the core of our being.

Mastery is when we are pure love in action. Love becomes the foundation of every thought and every action. Real or unconditional love is never wrong and will always be aligned with the good of the whole. Whether we are discussing a family or a corporation, love needs to be the universal thread woven into the tapestry of each moment. It should replace fear.

Chapter Four

What does self-mastery look, feel and sound like?

What will it look like when your team and their team and those people's teams have progressed in their self-mastery journey such that they become increasingly impervious to the daily dramas in the work place?

- A good, healthy morale will be maintained
- The work force will demonstrate a higher level of job satisfaction and effectiveness
- There will be greater harmony within work groups and among the organization
- There are less supervisors and managers and more leaders
- Leadership will spend less time with drama within their teams
- Leadership will spend less time with drama within the organization
- New ideas will be sprouting up on a routine basis and people will be taking more stock in their levels of accountability
- There will be a general feeling that people care and the staff will be productive
- Efficiency will improve and more people will want to be involved in process improvement because they will feel like a stake holder
- Unique and customary challenges are dealt with in a more positive manner and adverse outcomes have a shorter duration
- Stewardship becomes more visible within the organization and a commitment to community is broadened
- An organization begins to function in a similar fashion to a sacred community to help others, especially fellow team members, who are less fortunate or who experience extraordinarily difficult circumstances

- Staff unites their efforts in more global ways to improve or enrich the lives of others—what they give will come back a thousand fold or more
- Indices of financial success improve and more time is spent acting than worrying
- The "air" is lighter and filled with fulfillment and joy
- Customer/Client satisfaction is high and everyone is treated with respect and dignity
- The organization becomes an employer of choice
- The organization becomes a provider/supplier of choice

There are no disadvantages to exploring opportunities and promoting a consciousness of self-mastery in the work place. There is much work to do when a leader is committed to accelerating their self-mastery journey. It requires self-discipline and commitment to clear the clutter that forms the path of egoic thought and action. Doing the work from the inside-out will not only positively affect the workplace, it will have a dramatic influence on life. As relationships with the self improve, every other relationship improves, too. As leaders traverse this self-mastery terrain, the same opportunities should be afforded to everyone else, in a manner that is appropriate and professional. At times, it is difficult for companies to budget funds to assist in organizational development but I believe that is being penny wise and pound foolish. There is so much money lost on turnover, poor performance, adverse work environments, dysfunction and drama in the work place. Employees are a company's greatest asset and largest expense. It's as important to keep them whole in body/mind/spirit as it is updated on technical information and new discoveries. There will always be a percentage of staff that is not interested in improving themselves or changing the patterns of their thoughts. These people, however, will not be the most positive influences and highest performers. People who are not dedicated to the self-mastery journey are not ready to face the shadows of pain that reside within the levels of their consciousness. For example, anger may play a starring but inconspicuous role in their work day. Sometimes this anger lurks beneath the surface and is not readily observed. In time, that anger will float to the surface and given the power, will prevent the team from reaching its highest potential. Until people acknowledge their issues and become aware of how the subconscious mind rules the ego and sabotages our happiness and state of joyful living, we will continue to live in a quagmire of discomfort. The people who harbor their issues and maintain a fear of resolution deep in their core will not be the highest performers because they are not content with who they are and what they are getting out of life. They are often the alleged victims of a life that has treated them unfairly. It is often someone else's fault or they are victims of circumstance. They live a life that is drenched in unawareness. They are unaware of their lack of love for themselves and others and they are often unwilling to be accountable and accept the choices they have made. Self-mastery cannot occur without recognition that there are no victims in life. We are the authors and co-creators of our existence.

Mastery is the attainment of wisdom and the path to enlightenment. It is learning about the innate tools that we have to assist us in this journey. When a work place fosters individual self-mastery and promotes an environment of love and respect, the organization functions at a higher level of efficiency and harmony because of the sum of its parts. The following are signs of an individual's acceleration in their self-mastery journey that allow changes in the organization to occur:

- An individual will love and like themselves more every day
- A person appreciates their hands and feet and all that is in-between
- A person appears to bring light to people's lives and everyday situations, maintaining a positive attitude in the face of challenge
- The person who has excelled in the self-mastery journey lives their truth and kindness becomes the habit of the day
- An individual will seem to consistently see the beauty and goodness in people, situations and their surroundings
- They will become more service oriented
- An individual will desire to get involved to help make their community a better and more beautiful place to live
- A person will often crave alone time and will cherish the opportunities to sit quietly with the self in contemplation and/or meditation or prayer
- A person won't spend much time thinking about who was right and who was wrong and who thought of it first and who should get the credit
- With each passing day, a self-actualized person becomes more forgiving and non-judgmental of the self and therefore others
- It's common for people to apologize to this individual for comments or actions that didn't register with them or of which they have no recollection

- Those who know who they are and have traversed their self-mastery journey with love, contemplate and understand people's intentions instead of their words and external actions
- These people are more tolerant of human frailty, starting with themselves, and they maintain a constant awareness that everyone is doing the best they can given their current evolution of self
- These self-actualized people focus less on dogma and judgment and more on spirit
- The relationships and patterns of thoughts and actions that no longer serve this type of individual dissolve from their lives
- They often crave simplicity
- Negativity feels bad no matter the source or point of origination and they have the mind control to immediately take note of their egoic thoughts/fear and replace it with love
- There is less drama in these people's lives
- Everyone who hangs out with this type of person notices that their life seems to be taking on a greater ease and they are filled with joy
- These people put themselves first but they are not selfish and there is no guilt associated with this way of life as they give more love with each passing day
- This type of person no longer maintains a desire to *fix* everything in their life and the lives of others and understands the personal growth that is achieved from the trials and tribulations of life
- They no longer have a desire to be all things to all people and they hold themselves and others accountable
- They care more about what they think of themselves than of what others think of them
- They compete with themselves more than anyone else
- They care more deeply about the level of joy they experience and they are more likely to avoid doing things that do not bring them joy
- They may look and feel more healthy—even their relationship with food and exercise may seem different than it used to be
- These self-mastered people have less agendas and more adventures
- They have less fear
- When fear tries to rear its ugly head, they can quickly identify it and work to change their perspective to eliminate the emotions derived from those points of fear
- They don't hold grudges and they get over things faster

- The earth and all of nature takes on a greater and more intense beauty
- They laugh more
- They have a heightened love and compassion for all living things
- Within the self, there is a growing and incredible peace
- They understand "connections"
- During this life-long process, many of their favorites may have changed—clothing, colors, places to live, relationships, partnerships, foods, drink, recreation, etc.
- They feel the Universe's interconnectedness and each day they live in a more constant state of **oneness.**

Chapter Five

Alignment

To build a winning team, goals and objectives must be aligned for success. The best teams function through the sum of their individual powers of self-alignment. Simply, when a team member knows that they are in the right place, making a difference every day, doing something that is in their best interest and feels right in a complete kind of way, they will be in a state of self-alignment. In this state of self-alignment, a person will be an effective, efficient, and highly motivated team member. Said another way, a congruence exists that is felt in every part of one's being when they are self-aligned. The inside matches the outside—each a reflection of the other.

A great leader, therefore, builds the team with self-aligned individuals. To build this team, a leader must know what self-alignment looks, feels and sounds like, and most importantly, they must be self-aligned themselves.

The best organizational and personal alignments will be consistent with what is best for the whole. Success means different things to different people. The success I speak of is the success that will allow organizations to thrive and prosper and will allow employees to have harmonious and professionally and personally fulfilled work lives. At the same time, the organization will provide some good or service that helps to make the world a better place by contributing to the abundance of wealth and success that is not derived at the expense of harming anyone or anything. Here alignment has two fundamental variants. The first is ensuring that everyone understands the direction of which they're supposed to be working, hoping and dreaming. Although they may have a different place and responsibility in an organization, everyone should be able to visualize and speak the common goal. All employees must be able to move in the same direction being able to envision and understand the quest and the prizes. The second is that the culture of the organization must foster individual alignment—the alignment of oneself. Alignment of the self occurs when somebody is doing something that precipitates feelings of joy, confidence, commitment and love each day. The leader's role begins with hiring people that have the right skill set, a positive attitude, can do the job well and will enjoy what they're doing. All the square pegs will be in square holes, circular pegs will be in the circular holes and so on. When an employee comes to work every day and feels inadequate, their mood and ineffectiveness will bring the whole team down. When a leader allows this to continue, they become ineffective and the energy of a section, department, or organization slides downhill.

When an employee loves what they do at work but their personal lives are not in alignment with who they are, their work potential may or may not initially suffer, but in time, some level of dysfunction will surface. For example, if an employee feels their personal life sucks, they may still be a positive, productive influence at work for a time but the stress of the situation that sucks will eventually erode their resilience if they don't take control of their thoughts and feelings. The eventual dysfunction may manifest in an alteration of mood, attitude, productivity and in some cases, cause illness or dis-ease. Misalignment cannot occur forever without having some ill effect on a person. The manifestations of misalignment can also be contagious. Negative energy spreads and many do not have the inner tools to prevent suction into the negative swirl, thereby joining the vat of negativity and allowing it to grow and permeate. This happens at work, at home and everywhere in between. Although a leader should not be involved in the solving of personal problems, should a good employee begin to falter, there must be an opportunity for them to get assistance through the work place, since the work place should be their community of caring. This help could come from on site social workers or access to an Employee Assistance Program (EAP). It is not unusual for a leader to get wind of the downward spiral that one of their employees is travelling. A leader is someone who can relate to people and help provide that level of balance between professional and personal assistance. It's near impossible for anyone to separate their non-work thoughts, feelings and emotions from their work thoughts, feelings and emotions. Many have tried and may have done it for awhile, but eventually the intermingling and intertwining of this mind-body exchange merges. A good leader does not sit by and watch an employee struggle. They get involved to the level that is appropriate. To know what level is appropriate, one must be able to access this wisdom within the self. A great leader uses all five senses plus their intuition and with that sixth sense, will know what level of involvement is necessary and appropriate. Instead of reading a book that outlines the optimal mix of involvement in the lives of one's employees (which is impossible to articulate since every situation is different) a leader needs to be able to access their intuition, for the answers reside within the self. Those leaders stuck in their intellect will not be anywhere near as effective as a leader that uses all innate resources, including intuition. Those leaders stuck in their heads may laugh at this statement and I would just request them to perform their due diligence to explore the level of leadership success people who fire on all burners experience.

A great leader loves being a leader, as this honor and privilege is perfectly aligned with their soul mission to serve. If employee issues exhaust a leader and they really don't want to deal with or support anyone in a self-mastery journey, they should consider doing something else for a living. There is a magnitude of work to do on a daily basis but one of the most important roles of a leader is to mitigate frustration in the work place and facilitate progress. If people are employed and a department does not function solely on technology or robots, a leader will be dealing with personnel issues, like it or not. You have got to love it to do it—or a leadership role will be a drag that causes misalignment in the leader and when the leader is misaligned, where is anybody going?

When I was in 8th grade, I envied the boys who could take Industrial Arts class. They worked with wood and tools and machines and made things that were fun and could last a lifetime. We girls were the happy participants of "Home Economics." That was really fun, too. We learned how to sew and I made a great Raggedy Ann doll and several stuffed animals and pillows that my daughters still possess today. I wanted both opportunities, however, and it just didn't make sense to me that boys were the only ones who could take shop class? My father was a carpenter and I knew I must have been born with some wood-oriented gifts, so this passion gave birth to what I believe was a great idea. The last period of the day was a study hall and everyone knows most kids in 8th grade don't get much work done in study hall—well I didn't. I did my hours of homework at my desk in my bedroom, talking to myself such that my dad and brother often stopped in to see if anybody was with me! In any event, I gathered some opinions from my fellow girl and boy students to start an Industrial Arts Club. This club would be open to both boys and girls who elected to participate in the club instead of going to study hall. I spoke to the teacher, who spoke to the principal and my wish was granted. I thought it was important to have a President of this Industrial Arts Club and of course, I knew that should be me. I was the ideal candidate because it was my idea and I felt like I'd be a good leader. In fairness, however, I suggested the students interested in this position of leadership should be elected. That idea was embraced and the few of us who wanted to be the president campaigned, gave our speeches, and ran for office. As with most politicians, I did make a promise I had full intentions to fulfill, but never did. I had hoped I could organize a field trip, as I knew that would be an attractive campaign strategy. Time never permitted this trip but the Industrial Arts Club was a great success and several girls got to use the tools that heretofore only boys could utilize. I will always remember that I was the first girl at Columbus School in Utica, New York to ever use the jigsaw! It was a wonderful experience for me and I still have my wooden horse in my basement and in blue pencil on the bottom is written, 98%.

I always knew I would be a leader. My earliest recollection of this desire was when I was in 5th grade. A leader of what, I wasn't sure, but I knew I'd be a leader. I knew I didn't want to become a leader to tell people what to do; I felt a calling to serve. I knew I had it within myself to motivate other people and to make them laugh and feel good about themselves. I have always loved people, especially nice people. I have always disliked bullies and through my career, I've made every effort to assist in bully reformation or removal. I was also a good negotiator. That skill developed when I was around 14 years old, after the death of my mother. Subsequent to her death, I was living with two men— my father and brother. That was "Negotiation 101" for me. That experience appeared to enrich my persuasion skills at a young age. As life progressed, I discovered that I had a knack for planting seeds in other people's minds that would eventually sprout into ideas that were consistent with my desires, too. One can say this is also called, manipulation, and in a way, I agree. When the intentions are for the good of the whole, however, and not related to personal agendas or power, I think the skill is valuable. When my mom died, I had to grow up fast and live in a man's world. That was the best training for my leadership career—as most of my early years of leadership were lived in a "man's world." That paradigm is changing now and that is good as the world of opportunity should be based on the content of character and gifts. From an energetic perspective, my perception of a "man's world" relates to the characteristics of masculine energy. I am confident that we're heading into a day when there will be a balance and blend of feminine and masculine energy, for I believe this will be the energy of successful and joy filled organizations in the future. This energy has nothing to do with being male or female. The energy relates to the characteristics and fundamental philosophies of thought. It's not my intention to review metaphysical characteristics of masculine and feminine energy, but suffice to say, if a person takes time to think about it, I'm confident they can delineate the two. The balance of that energy is imperative in a cohesive and successful work environment.

At 14 years of age, the worst thing that could possibly happen to me . . . did. Watching my mother lie in a hospital bed for months and watching her die catapulted my ability to handle stress and become resilient. Feeling and knowing that my mom was still with me after she died catapulted my spirituality and introduced me to a world of spirit that I could trust. If I wasn't sure that we were a spirit having a physical experience before she died, I was 100% certain thereafter. Oddly enough, her death was one of the greatest tragedies and gifts of my life.

Leadership feeds my soul. It is an honor and I maintain a great reverence for the rights and privileges associated with any level of leadership. My first leadership opportunity occurred when I was 24 years old and it didn't take me long to realize that I had lost as many privileges as I had gained. There could be no more bad moods, getting angry, complaining about management, being negative and so on. A leader sets the tone and the tone must be loving, positive, accountable, equitable and inspiring for people to work in harmony and want to come to work. Another important right you lose as a leader is to be misaligned for any length of time. A leader has a responsibility to continue on the self-mastery journey to clear the clutter in their minds that prevents them from being a pure and open channel of great leadership.

With this first management experience, Friday, I was among my peers and colleagues and the next Monday, I was their supervisor. That was an interesting introduction to leadership. My first staff meeting was attended by my three employees and me. The four of us were very cozy in a small little office in the back of a laboratory. One of the employees, the most senior with the most experience, decided he would ignore me and read a magazine at the commencement of the meeting. I was 24 years old and I wanted to jump out of my chair and punch him in the face. Obviously, my self-mastery journey was in its infancy! Instead, I took a deep breath, stopped any discussion, put a hold on the start of the meeting and waited for him to look up. When he did, I just asked if what he was reading was interesting and relevant to the meeting and if so, I welcomed him to share it with us before we got started. He just smiled and put the magazine down. That is when I knew that a leader had to forfeit their right to lose their temper. If I were to be successful, I had to embrace this new way of work life. The interesting thing about this story is that this employee sort of became my friend and we developed a genuine respect for one another. This would be my first irritant and mirror in my life of leadership to teach me what was inside of myself. I have a great deal of gratitude for this individual, as he taught me a lot about being a good leader.

We surround ourselves with people—friends, co-workers, family members and strangers that act as mirrors to reflect that which we choose or choose not to see within ourselves. People illuminate things about ourselves that we may love or loathe. The lens of which we choose to view others is dependent upon the lens we use to view ourselves. When we are critical of everything we do, we will be critical of others. When others can't meet our expectations it's often because we're so engrossed in meeting our own expectations and preparing for the worst. We often place expectations on others and assume they will react the way we desire, when we have no right to do that, and will be disappointed more times than not. When we continually fail to meet our expectations, we develop anger that can be displaced to other people. It's easy to feel guilty about our lack of perfection. It's also common to worry in advance so the next time we fail to meet our expectations, we'll be prepared. People spend so much time in the past and future that they lose sight of the present, the now. When we are tolerant of ourselves and accept that when we do our best, our best is good enough, we become tolerant to human frailty and that will ultimately promote an inner peace and harmony. Wasn't it Pollyanna that said, "When you look for the good in people expecting to find it, you surely will?" OK—maybe it was Abraham Lincoln, but when I was little, I felt closer to Pollyanna. When we choose to remove the residual dust off the mirror that people provide to us, we choose to look inside and clear the clutter that causes the day to day chatter that often sabotages our desire to be happy and do well. When our eyes are filled with love, love is what we see and we can develop a genuine appreciation for ourselves and others.

Every thought we have and every decision we make stems from what we think about ourselves. The value we place on ourselves is represented in every relationship we have. It is imperative for a leader to understand who they are and to gain control over their mental and emotional bodies. As with everyone, what resides on the inside shines forth for the world to see on the outside. Our lives become a reflection of the quality of our thoughts and the extent of love that permeates our being.

If you made a list of the biggest irritants in your life—those individuals that drove you crazy, pushed your buttons, tested your resilience and instigated fear, anger or anxiety within you—I'm confident you could complete that list by articulating the gifts those people provided to you in your life. The elements of truth about yourself they elucidated were gifts. The skills you developed from knowing those individuals and overcoming challenge were gifts. One of the greatest gifts someone can provide to us is the gift of learning and training ourselves to be impervious. When we have to put forth great effort to not let somebody affect our mood or our way of life, we learn self-control and self-mastery. We learn how to control our emotions—to let things go and not get attached to comments or behaviors of other people. We recognize that the clutter that resides within those people drives the characteristics of their behavior. The outside is a reflection of the inside. One must recognize that the words and actions of the irritants result from the value they place on themselves. The irritant, however, may ruffle the feathers that reside within the self because they dust off the self-reflecting mirror that illuminates similar characteristics. An adverse reaction to somebody may occur because a person dislikes the characteristics of the irritant that come into focus. Many times, these characteristics resonate at some level of consciousness to strike a familiar chord within. These could be old ways that have been healed and resolved. It's also possible that similarities with the irritant highlight those characteristics that still reside within the self and have not been eliminated to date. Our irritants teach us that the only control we have is the control over ourselves. We learn that the only person responsible for our happiness is our self. We learn that honest communication with the self is imperative.

Alignment, when focused upon, can be felt at every level of our being. We can feel it physically, mentally, emotionally and spiritually. Physically, mal-alignment manifests in such ways as headaches, neck pain, back pain, stomach aches, and other mild or severe stress related ailments. Mentally and emotionally, mal-alignment manifests as self-talk, that incessant internal discussion that reminds us that we're not happy by picking everything apart. Self-talk results when we're in a mode to analyze the words, actions and motives of ourselves and others. Self-talk can be judgmental, critical and hurtful. When a person gives life to these rational or irrational thoughts, a cascade of emotions ensue that affect mood and actions—and sometimes physical health and well-being. Spiritually, when people are not happy, there is often some sort of void or lack of fulfillment. They may feel a type of emptiness or lack of support and love. They may feel there is something they're missing in life and they may feel a palpable disconnection. At times, their spiritual life may become more external and less internal. They may hang on to religion for dear life but fail to recognize the divinity within the self and others. Misalignment may foster the separateness of our existence rather than the unity and oneness. A victim role is often developed and people forget they hold their deck of cards and they have free will to shuffle and play them. The fact that they co-created this plan often eludes them and they blame anything and everything on factors outside of themselves, instead of looking inside. Co-created plans are discussed in detail in Chapter Ten but I am referring to the life plan that we co-authored prior to our birth and we continue to author with every thought and choice we make. The trials, tribulations and celebrations that we placed and continue to place in our life plan proceed for the purpose of ultimate growth and spiritual development. Re-alignment fosters resiliency. We can do anything we put our minds to because we have all the tools necessary to be happy and successful.

In summary, life just doesn't feel right when what we are thinking and doing is not aligned with our highest good and is inconsistent with our soul journey. During those times when we're not happy, we must inquire within and ask ourselves the difficult questions. If something does not bring you joy, why would anyone feel it necessary to continue doing it? Do the answers point to a lack of self-love and courage to speak our truth and make changes in our lives? When we're doing what we love and what is aligned with our soul's journey, it feels right. It's a feeling of inner peace and provides a level of conscious satisfaction. Discomfort speaks volumes and is an essential mechanism by which our internal auditor communicates with us. It's important for us to evaluate feelings of discomfort when related to our jobs or anything else and it's important to ask oneself why choose to be unhappy and live in this discomfort.

When a person is not happy at their job, they have two choices. They can get a new job or change their mind about the job. If a person hates their job but is in it for the money and getting a new job is not an option, an essential ingredient of mastery is to have the capacity and mind control to change their perspective about the job. A person would need to find something to love about it or the reasons for its existence and purpose in their life. If there is nothing to love but the money, then gratitude for the money needs to replace the feelings of misery. There will be something to be grateful for if you look and that feeling of gratitude and self-love must replace the thoughts that produce the misery. There is always a reason for the challenge, as things are not always what they appear to be. When we know we can't change a situation, the only thing we can count on is having the wisdom to change our mind so we can sustain in peace. When we know we must move on, we need to have the confidence and faith that we will be lead to where we can make a difference. We must recognize our power and believe in our ability to redirect or reinvent ourselves whenever we need it.

Chapter Six

Know your "Credit Score"

There is great interest in credit scores these days but the credit score I am referring to has nothing to do with Equifax, TransUnion, or Experian's numerical expression of people's creditworthiness. It is about an aspect of fear that may be seen in any department, work group, family and community. It has everything to do with a person's level of apprehension to share ideas and contribute to the success of the whole for fear that they won't earn the credit they believe they deserve. It can also be associated with people who share snippets of a whole bunch of ideas but can't make anything come to fruition because they don't want any of their ideas to pan out unless everybody can see that they were an integral part of the reason for success. There can be varying levels of this characteristic within people, from mild and hardly noticeable to overt and obstructive. The self-mastery journey will provoke the identification of these characteristics deeply seeded in an individual, for it is a lack of self-love and confidence that creates the manifestations of activity referred to in this chapter. In the self-mastery journey, a person evaluates how credit and control alter their thoughts and actions, both at work and in their everyday life. People will realize that they need to assess people and their performance themselves. A lazy or insecure leader may take a new position and latch on to some person who they think will provide insight as to whose performance is exceptional, adequate or inadequate. It's fine to listen and gather input but a leader must assess performance themselves. A good leader hears all perceptions but creates their own impressions and makes decisions about performance themselves.

Credit cravers come in all shapes, sizes and varieties and reside at every level in an organization. These credit loving leaders and employees have as much beauty inside as anyone else, they just can't always see it or the magnitude of its depth. They are actually working from a position of limitation instead of potential. It is not unlikely that someplace along the way, somebody made them feel like no matter what they do or how they do it, it's not good enough. They may be totally oblivious to the level of attention and accolades they need to feel good about themselves. These credit lovers are a close cousin to importance loving people. These are the leaders and employees who need to look important. Their focus is handicapped because of their insecurities. Energy will be expended on things that are a waste of time. Confident, self-assured leaders and employees don't care or worry about looking important. They feel important already and they focus on getting the job done as best as they can. They are more consumed with the progress and quality of the team and the output. Smart, effective leaders will be recognized by most. Good leaders don't speak it, they live it. Those who feel a need to remind others that they are in positions of authority need to examine what's deep inside, precipitating this need. The self-mastery journey asks these difficult questions of leaders and fosters an environment for people to look within and gain the self-love and confidence to go forward as a leader, knowing and believing in themselves. It sheds light on a person's desire to be someone or something that is not consistent with who they are and may lead them in a different direction. A direction that is more aligned with who they are and what is in their highest good. It's not a failure to learn that a leadership role is not what's meant to be—it is a redirection to become more happy and fulfilled.

The care that credit loving people take in spreading themselves around to make sure they're involved in everything detours their energy from that of a successful venture to that of a cat chasing their tail. In the process of chasing their tail, there will be miscommunication and apprehension as to the true intent of the individual. When a person gets stuck in worrying about who will get the credit for an idea or implementation or whatever the circumstance may be, the conscious or subconscious fear that is fueling their burners becomes the dominant energy of expression. If somebody worries enough about getting the credit, they may not speak up for fear that their ideas may be stolen. Another possibility is the inadvertent sabotage of the efforts of others. This type of behavior, in addition to other manifestations of needing and wanting credit, eventually propagates a reputation of somebody who can't be trusted. The people who don't trust this individual, however, may not be able to articulate exactly why that is the case, due to the subtleness of the interference. When people are consumed with protecting their ideas, hording knowledge and getting credit, they manipulate circumstances to their benefit and it becomes more about them than the good of the whole. It may not be the intent in their hearts and minds, but their actions become misunderstood by the people. With time, this can surface as the appearance of hidden agendas. This perception of the work group may slowly instigate mistrust and misunderstandings. It will look like those who are consumed with getting recognition and credit are self centered, untrustworthy people whereas the reality is that their perception of self is skewed and they need those accolades to cover what is really going on inside themselves. Instead of doing the work by traveling within to clear the clutter that prevents those types of people from seeing the beauty and perfection within themselves, they unconsciously look for the feel good cover-up. A person whose number one priority is to look good, ensure their due credit and wow the group can ultimately become the big loser. This "me-me-me" behavior is really a call for help, as the person is wallowing in a lack of self-confidence and a belief that they are not good enough. When a person continually functions from this place of fear, everyone loses. If it persists with continuous negative outcomes, this credit loving individual will become the type of employee who loses their job but can't truly understand the reasons. The termination will be inevitable because ultimately the other staff members will lose trust and respect. This loss of trust and respect will result from the chords of fear that are struck within the people who are affected by the credit craving person. A group of highly evolved team members will see the cover-up and know that an aspect of self-worth, deep in the heart of that credit monger isn't based in self-love. They may find it in their hearts to give the person time to inquire within and do the work necessary to learn where these credit cravings originate and when and where the source of this addiction was created. This wait can get exhausting, however, and cause good energy to be wasted because of the dysfunction. In time, most will get sick of waiting and be done with it. For some, a mere awareness of their credit craving will awaken them out of this groove and the situation will resolve. The choice rests solely with that individual as they will control their destiny.

A good leader must become the team's role model by relinquishing their need for credit. That tone must be a fundamental component of what they expect from the work group. Credit cannot be the focus. This isn't something that is usually talked about—it's a way of life. As life would have it, credit comes to those who deserve it and a good leader always reaps the rewards of a highly functioning and successful team. In some form or another, the Universe maintains all records, so it takes keeping score off of our job description.

Good leadership will foster partnerships and teamwork without hierarchy. What box a person resides in on the org chart should not be the stimulus for accolades and credit. When the team is successful, everyone is successful. When a team member lags behind, everyone lags behind. This fundamental style will encourage everyone to work together, assist those that need help and encourage those who are square pegs in round holes to move on to a more suitable position. The people whose energy is self-serving will likely self-select out of the organization. They will seek a job in which they feel more comfortable and fit in.

Whatever we focus on will expand and people will attract what lies in their dominate thoughts. If an organization is only about money, it will attract the type of person who vibrates to that frequency and whose focus is on money. If it's a cut throat organization, it will attract cut throat workers who feel comfortable and motivated in that environment. The tone for this will be set by the thoughts and actions from the top down. Every organization develops a personality. That personality is made by the collective consciousness of the people who make it up. The leader at the top has to decide what is important and what kind of people they want working for the company. They will need to communicate with all leaders so everyone is clear on the fundamental character traits desired of the people. Each person who maintains responsibility to hire people will need to have the same understanding.

A leader sets the tone and standard for the behavior they expect of the people they lead, by the example they set. The good works of the team should never be invisible and credit needs to be given to individuals as well as the whole. Honest feedback should be provided at all times. I can't recall being successful at anything in all the years of my work, without that success being interrelated or even dependent upon the work of others. Since I have enjoyed high level leadership roles for much of my career, I can honestly say that when it comes to daily successes, I was the least important person involved—as it should be.

While a leader is working hard, not paying attention to how much credit they are receiving, credit continues to pour in. It's similar to, "it is in giving that we receive." Everyone wins as they get the credit for high performance. The more you don't ask for it—the more you get it. The Universe always knows of one's contributions to the world, and those contributions come back a thousand fold.

Control is another manifestation of fear that is a close cousin to credit. We're still dealing with fear and the perceived threatening of a person's value, worth or security. A person must look within to evaluate the role that control plays in their work and everyday life. Let's address the personality style that needs to control all projects, reports, contracts, budgets, spending, etc. When we accept the statement that every relationship depends on the relationship we have with ourselves, we can gather inside information from this desire to control. The desire for control is interrelated to our ability to trust. If a leader does not trust themselves, it will be near impossible for them to trust other people. Unless an organization only needs one person to do everything, the ability to trust others is paramount. What makes a person want to control every aspect of a proposal, project, job or even department? The micromanager may feel a personal responsibility to minimize the potential for error to an irrational degree. This failure to trust others incites paralysis from the fear they instill in subordinates. The control oriented leader may believe they are smarter than anyone and nobody can do a job as well as them. My response would be, "Think again—as you should be hiring people as smart or smarter than yourself." If not smarter, a more well defined expertise in their area of work. The control oriented leader may think they are accountable for other's thoughts and deeds and they may get overwhelmed by their perceived role. This overwhelmed individual could shift into control mode in an attempt to alleviate the stress that results from their fear of failure. They may think if they can gather all their responsibilities onto one plate and keep them in view, they will be safe. This type of leader, however, may also be totally oblivious to what's really going on inside of them and just accept the internal stress as an occupational hazard. This type of control oriented leader may also be very fearful of their boss and may be afraid they will lose their job if they fail. Unfortunately or fortunately, this type of redirection is a part of life and if anyone really expects perfection at every turn, they should be self-employed with no employees. If a superior induces such pressure and fear, and there is no hope that their inadequacy will result in their termination, then the person reporting to them has some serious evaluating to perform. They may be doing themselves a huge disservice in this position. If both the supervisor and subordinate have a tendency to control things at work, this mix will become toxic to everyone in their path. There are many reasons why a person possesses the insecurities to want to control everything. Only the person who possesses the desire to control can really figure out the source of this insatiable desire. As we can only control ourselves, it's understandable that the feeling to control other people and situations would be extremely stressful and exhausting. Perhaps the micromanager is fearful that an error would blemish their pristine record of perfection. When we expect perfection we will always fall short.

It is always possible that a subordinate will make a decision that lacks the finest of judgment. Unless a leader wants to perform every job, that's the chance that both the average leader and the outstanding leader takes. This chance is only mitigated by hiring the right people and trusting them to do their best. When the right people are selected for a job, their best will always be good enough. A micromanager makes people crazy because their judgment and leadership style are based in fear. They have an incredible need to monitor and control everything and this makes the people around them nuts. It often requires subordinates to provide such detail that the magnitude of their job is consumed with activities not related to getting the job done, but in creating a level of exhausting minutia that makes the micromanager feel better. These leaders are often risk averse so it's highly likely that after all the effort and aggravation, in the end, the group will be exhausted and the success level will fall dramatically short from where it could be if trust and empowerment were the energies that drove the process. Great leaders will not work for control freak micromanagers. They value their time and talent too much. Putting a micromanager at the top of the food chain is a recipe for mediocrity, dysfunction and an organization that will miss the true mark of success. The blood, sweat and tears of the micromanager and their subordinates will be drowned in detail and real progress will never occur. It may take 5–10 years to retrospectively see this tragedy but in time, the lack of creativity, risk and trust will be to the demise of the organization. People will wonder what happened—especially if this micromanager is extremely intelligent and a nice person. Not everyone will be able to recognize fear based energy. The lack of success will surely not be due to a lack of hours that people put in—as the details often take well over 40–50 hours a week to complete.

A leader enriches the trust they have in themselves by knowing that they have the tools to perform well. To know this, a leader may have to heal aspects of their belief system that may have been developed early in their life. They must also have confidence in their ability to hire the right people to do the job and relinquish uncertainty and control. A leader needs to ensure that those who report to them have skills that will also complement the gifts they possess. It's important to ensure that the team is comprised of people who possess the array of characteristics needed to accomplish any task successfully. Global perspectives, strategic insights, and attention to detail are some of the characteristics needed by the sum of the whole. Intuition is a great tool because it allows for the transmission of information from a higher order. If the leader's rule of action is to always function from the position of what is best for the whole, intuitive insights can assist in ways that foster genuine success. There will be challenges and frustrations or it wouldn't be life, but the release of egoic, earthly, control oriented philosophies will be astoundingly helpful. Trusting in oneself and in an infrastructure that is not seen but is here to serve can assist in putting the right people in the right places for the highest good.

Intuition plays an important role in the hiring of people. It is critical to understand the qualifications of a position and interview candidates who meet the criteria of skill level, academic training and experience. Once you have choices of qualified individuals, intuition can help nudge the selection of the best candidate. During my career, I have always used my intuition when hiring an individual. During an interview, when the successful candidate presents, my intuition always lets me know. I have never made a bad choice. I have hired people that didn't work out for various reasons and I've had to terminate them, but the human interaction was always meant to be and there was always growth on every side—mine, the coworkers and the person I hired and fired. Even if a person you hire ends in a termination, there was a reason for the experience and exchange. There are no accidents or bad choices—there is growth. Growth doesn't always feel good, but everything that happens is for our highest good.

When you love and trust yourself to hire the right people, there is no need for micromanagement or control. Expectations for the employee should be clear, the appropriate training and tools to be successful given, and the employee should be let free to create, love and produce. In a loving and effective leadership climate, when an employee approaches their limits of comfort with any decision or detail, or they just need advice, they will know and feel comfortable to approach their leader without fear of any kind. Communication and access are critical but involving oneself in minutia is counterproductive.

A leader attracts the same or similar vibration of consciousness as their own. The ideals, values and characteristics they focus upon will expand. For that reason, a leader should live in the consciousness of love and think and create the existence they desire for themselves and their organization. Their intuition should be their guide when it comes to looking in the eyes of their colleagues and employees to see the souls that will allow for the propagation of an effective and harmonious team. They must love what they do for without love, there will not be true success.

Chapter Seven

The Vibration of Leadership

Perhaps it is unusual to relate the word vibration to leadership, but metaphysically, it's a great way to understand why leadership is more a way of life than a role we play while we're at work. Everyone is a leader in some form, even if the only form recognized is the manner in which a life lived becomes an example to others. The self-mastery journey is very much related to vibration because it is related to love and light at the most fundamental levels. It is essential to understand the roles that vibration, energy, light and love play in our lives.

Although we may not give this much thought, everything in the Universe vibrates. The huge and heavy redwood trees are vibrating. The table of which I'm using to hold my laptop while I write this book is vibrating. I'm vibrating and so are you. You can do a web search on quantum physics, the string theory, quarks and more to read about all the scientific evidence that substantiates the vibration of everything in our Universe. I'll leave the scientific evidence to the experts and I'll just speak about my own empirical data, conclusions and scientific principles I've learned along the way in my scholarly journey. If you have a hard time relating leadership to vibration, think of it metaphorically and we should still end up on the same page.

The highest vibrations in the Universe are the vibrations of love, pure unconditional love and gratitude. In comparison, the vibration of fear is of a low or dense vibration. If you want to feel what exposure to those vibrations feels like to the physical body, silence your mind, take a deep breath, close your eyes and think of someone you love the very most. See them, feel them and take them into your heart. See them smile and laugh and allow every cell in your body to vibrate in love. How does that feel? Take note of where the feelings are located in your body. Pay attention to every emotion and feeling produced. I'm confident it feels great. This euphoric feeling of love can be produced instantaneously by using the power of our minds. You can picture people, nature, scenery that you love, sounds and smells that touch your heart, anything that fosters feelings of love and gratitude. This is a tiny example of what the vibration of love can produce. Imagine how life would be if everyone on the planet could "hold" that position of love for themselves and everyone and everything else!

Perform the same procedure as outlined in the previous paragraph, using thoughts of something that scares you to your core—think of one of your greatest fears. Live in that fear for a few moments—exaggerate what you're afraid of and let it play in your mind for a bit of time. Pay close attention to where and how the fear feels in your body. Among other feelings, you may have a sick feeling in the pit of your stomach, your heart may be beating more rapidly and you may even feel your body becoming heavy and dense and tired. That is how we respond to the vibration of fear, and fear exists at a magnitude of levels, many of which we are not consciously aware. Some live in the vibration of fear. Some leaders live in the vibration of fear. Fear of inadequate performance, fear of not having the respect they believe they deserve, fear of not being important or looking important enough, fear of failure and/or fear of getting fired. This vibration, at some level of consciousness, will be recognized by every individual who comes in contact with that physical, mental, emotional, and spiritual energy. In time, it will affect many of the decisions a person makes and it can and will sabotage the efforts of the team. Carrying fear over to everyday life, the decisions fear catalyses can also sabotage relationships outside of work. Partnerships, families and friendships are not immune to fear. Whether people are cognizant of it or not, fear will attempt to play a dramatic role in life. People may or may not be consciously aware of what's going on and what energy is fueling interactions. It is therefore essential for leaders to maintain a level of vibration that promotes their own health and well-being, in addition to promoting an atmosphere of harmony and production. Said another way, the vibration of leadership that is desired is a form of love. That vibration of love—love of self, the good of the whole, the people, the organization, the world and the Universe—feeds the souls of all involved. This vibration is essential and it cannot be truly integrated into one's being unless that vibration is a way of life and not a temporary desire to be effective or happy at work.

Some people refer to this vibration of love as God. This would substantiate the fact that whatever form of God one believes in, we are God and God is us. For the people who don't believe in God, per se, perhaps a belief in kindness, goodness, and awe for this complex, abundant, and precious Universe suffices. No matter how you slice it, love is the fundamental theme that must be integrated into our being, and we all need it, want it and search for it. Being filled with love, makes for a good person, a good employee, a good leader, a good owner, a good anything. When we see that this common thread weaves us together and is the one element of life essential to everyone and everything, we begin to have an understanding of how we are all one. We recognize our connectedness and we begin to see, believe and know that love has no production boundaries. From a happy home life to peace on earth, love is the answer. We use our free will every day to decide how we're going to think and feel and act. Life changes from moment to moment, and change is a constant in everyone's life, but the power of our thoughts and our ability to choose our thoughts never changes. We are all in control of how we think and we can decide for love or fear in every moment of every day. Irrespective of everything that has happened to us in our lifetime, we are a victim of nothing and no one. We made choices and decisions to come to earth, the land of density and opportunity, to learn to love. This consciousness of the Universe, when comprised of the aggregate of everyone's love for themselves and others, knows no boundaries. When we are tingling and overflowing with love, we feel a euphoric sense of joy, inner peace and a knowing of the mystery and power that resides within us.

Albert Einstein, through his mathematical equation, $E = mc^2$, proved that anything that has mass is energy and that energy and mass are dual expressions of the same Universal substance. That Universal substance is the energy or vibration of which we are composed. Albert Einstein viewed humans as a network of complex energy fields. He believed that these energy fields are connected at physical and cellular levels. Knowing that we are beings of energy, we can view our lives in ways related to energy and vibration—that primal substance that makes us who we are. We can view our health and well-being from an energetic standpoint and we can begin to comprehend the energy and vibration related to our thoughts and actions from that viewpoint as well.

We are electromagnetic beings in that we have numerous electrical systems operating in our human body. We know, for example, that the electricity of the heart can be measured by an Electrocardiogram (ECG or from the German derivative Elektrokardiogramm EKG). A law in Physics, known as Ampere's Law, states that whenever an electric current flows through human tissue, an electromagnetic field is created. Since we have numerous electrical systems in our bodies, we have a significant electromagnetic field around us. This is most easily exemplified when we don't hear somebody enter a room but we can "feel" them. We often get uncomfortable when somebody invades our space and gets too close to our bodies. We rarely picture the mingling of our magnetic fields and realize that the discomfort we are experiencing may be felt from physical, emotional, mental or spiritual levels. It is also an accepted principle in physics that different frequencies can peacefully coexist in the same space. By that, I mean different frequencies can occupy the same space or areas without destroying one another. We see this with radio and TV stations—just because we turn the receiver to connect to a different frequency doesn't mean the other frequencies are not there anymore.

In addition to heart rhythms, and TV and radio signals, there are many other examples of vibration that we may not have given thought to lately. One is our sight and our ability to see colors. Another is sound and our ability to hear. I always loved blowing in dog whistles when I was a kid. I never had a dog and I always wondered if they worked. No matter how hard I blew, I never heard a sound and dogs never came running. I learned much later in life that they do make a sound, but the sound is outside our human capacity to hear that frequency. I can't forget to mention our cell phones and texting. Brain activity is another excellent example of vibration that can be measured by performing an electroencephalogram or EEG.

In medicine, there are many forms of energy used in the diagnosis and treatment of disease. X-rays, MRI, CT, PET imaging devices all use forms of energy. Linear Accelerators used for Radiation treatments in cancer patients utilize energy to destroy cancer cells. Many people would not be alive without pacemakers and defibrillators, two pieces of instrumentation that rely on energy for their use. Everything in the body vibrates. *Wheels of Light: Chakras, Auras, and the Healing Energy of the Body* is a book written by Rosalyn L. Bruyere. In her book, she writes about studies that have shown that cancer cells vibrate at a lower frequency than healthy cells. She states that a cancerous cell is a low-frequency cell that does not vibrate at the same rate as the body but instead, vibrates at a much slower frequency.

If you have ever had any energy work, like Reiki or Therapeutic Touch or Healing Touch, or had Acupuncture, these modalities work on the energetic systems in our bodies called chakras and meridians. The vibration and spinning of open chakras can be demonstrated by placing a pendulum over the part of the body where they reside. The pendulum will rotate in the direction of the open chakra, usually clockwise (when the person is laying face up/on their back). There are colors and pitches also associated with the chakra system, all related to their vibration and the rate that produces the different colors and harmonics.

One of the most dramatic and easy to understand pictorial representations of the vibrational energy of human thoughts and intentions has been gifted to us by a Japanese scientist named Dr. Masaru Emoto. His work with water crystals is well known and he has authored many wonderful books that show the results of years of his research. In his books you will find that his discovery has been reproduced all over the world for many years. He has proven that human vibrational energy, thoughts, words, ideas and music affect the molecular structure of water. He demonstrated that when water molecules were exposed to vibrations and energy such as pollution, negative thoughts or intentions, or heavy metal/chaotic music, amorphous structures without any form of crystalline formation were observed. On the flip side, however, when water molecules were exposed to loving thoughts or intentions, prayer, or serene music, these vibrations created incredibly lovely crystals. To me, these crystals look similar to beautiful snowflakes. One of the quotes that I love from Dr. Emoto is, "Words are an expression of the soul. The condition of our soul is very likely to have an enormous impact on the water that composes our body—and this impact does not effect our bodies in a small way." I am fascinated by his discoveries but I'm not surprised because I maintain a strong personal belief in the extraordinary power of our thoughts and intentions. I always say, everything is about vibration. Since about 70% of our bodies and our earth are comprised of water, it makes a lot of sense how the collective consciousness of our thoughts can affect our families, our workplaces, our communities, our nation and our world.

Having shared all this information, let's get back to the vibration of leadership. Perhaps you have an idea where I'm going now as I relate energy and vibration to leadership. The vibration of leadership is one of self-love, coupled with a commitment to make any work place the best it can be through the cumulative efforts of every person involved. Just like the only person we can control is ourselves, the only person who can truly influence our vibration is ourselves. As with every person, the goal of any leader should be to vibrate to the highest frequency they can achieve, while supporting and fostering an environment where others can do the same. It's essential to empower every worker to be the best they can be—while facilitating and embracing a culture that allows them to find the divinity and perfection within themselves, if they choose to look. Like any fabric that maintains a consistent pattern, the fundamental elements of leadership must be woven into the being of a leader such that their global outlook, daily perspective and ability to make wise decisions come naturally. Wisdom and intuitive skill can be called upon at any time without preparation or planning. The vibration of leadership is that pattern of thought that maintains a quality of light and love throughout its product. The characteristics of a good leader become more evident through the progression of the self-mastery journey as self-love and self-realization continue to evolve and become enriched. Self-realization is the process by which we as humans remember our Divine nature and awaken our knowing of the wisdom of the Universe found within the recesses of our mind, body and spirit. Self-realization is understanding the role of our thoughts in the creation of our lives and the power within ourselves to access wisdom of the world and answers to our questions. When we journey this path, we gain a level of self-control and self-understanding that resides at the deepest levels of our being. As this love fest grows, our self-confidence catapults and our fears and hidden agendas melt away. When we are a being who comes from a place of love, instead of fear, our ability to trust, take risk, and produce skyrockets. True leadership is not something you turn on and off, it's who you are at all times. The vibration of leadership needs to be fed with courage and commitment. The denseness of negativity must be shed to illuminate the hope and opportunity that always exists in every challenge.

A leader makes a decision to be happy and filled with love during their work day, in the same fashion they make that decision the rest of the time. There is no separation of work and home when one understands that they are the only person in control of their happiness. Our level of happiness exists as a result of our decision to look at the blessings in life, maintain an attitude of appreciation, gratitude and love, and be happy. Some days the decision to be happy is more difficult than others, but it's always a decision. Expectations that anyone at home or at work can make us a happy person are sure to be followed by disappointment. Placing expectations on others, thinking we can control situations and people and giving life to false interpretations are egoic expressions of thought that lead us away from a joyful and peace filled existence.

Organizations have an associated vibration, too. It's comprised of the sum of its parts and can be felt by employees and visitors. Have you ever walked into a store or doctor's office or any type of business and "felt the vibe?" Have you ever gone for an interview and knew the job was not for you because you could feel it? A college campus is another good example. At a conscious or unconscious level, the potential student evaluates this aspect of college life during the campus visit. The vibration of an organization is sensed and it affects all workers, clients, visitors, etc. This recognition may occur on a conscious or unconscious basis, but it occurs. In time, this vibration fosters a reputation.

Just as our refrigerator magnets are magnetized to stick, humans are magnetized by the quality of their thoughts, such that they will draw like thoughts, ideas and circumstances to themselves. The electromagnetic force that is created from the variety of electrical systems occurring in our bodies sets up a perfect magnetic medium for our thoughts to exist and follow Universal laws, such as the "Law of Attraction." When we think love we attract love, when we think negatively, we attract more of the same. The electromagnetic field provides another sense and we can learn to feel and trust our instincts to intuit and feel a person's body language and vibe.

Perhaps you are familiar with the vibration of "slime?" The world is filled with variations, the yin and yang of existence. Instead of saying something is good or bad, I think it's better to express it as "it just is"— as things are not always what they appear to be and it is not in our best interest to label the aspects of life. If we look at everything as occurring for our highest good and growth, even situations, events and relationships we feel are not good for us and don't feel right, serve a purpose. In chapter nine, when we explore the value of discomfort, we will see the remarkable purpose discomfort plays our life, as it is one of our greatest innate communication tools. A leader must develop a keen awareness to the vibration of slime. This is the density that one feels when they are with someone who is dishonest, lacks integrity and self-respect and the respect of others or is driven by selfish needs as opposed to the good of the whole. I think of a person who vibrates at the frequency of slime as perhaps somebody motivated by power and money who tries to disguise their true nature by covering themselves with a blanket of deceit. The blanket will not mask their true vibration. If a person ever feels like they need to wash their hands after meeting somebody, tune into your intuition and try to consciously articulate why that feeling exists. Like vibrations attract, this includes the attraction of slime to slime. Opposing vibrations repel, this includes the repelling of slime to goodness. I make every attempt to recognize slime and stay away from it—the business deals I hope to make are with like minded individuals that vibrate to the frequency of fairness and goodness. As we continue to develop our intuitive nature, our ability to detect variations in the types of vibration improves. We will attract what we desire when it resonates with our individual vibration.

So many people are looking for proof. Many maintain a consistent desire for every hypothesis they integrate into their life to be proven by science. I love when science substantiates what I know to be true, too, but I am open minded to a world that is unseen and unknown. When scientific proof exists, faith is not required. Faith is an aspect of love that increases our vibration. When we inquire within and use our intuition, this sense of knowing and self-realization allows us to draw our conclusions and form our belief systems. When we think love, the vibration of love precipitates exponential increases in the vibrational state of which we live. This concept offers a comparison between how I view religion and spirituality. Religion is something that was taught to me in the same fashion—using the same words and dogmas that were used to teach my parents and their parents and so on. For me, religion is external and spirituality is internal. Spirituality is something that cannot be taught but it can be inspired and felt. Spirituality is that vibration and level of awakening that occurs within that allows us to not only believe but to know that we are a part of something greater. It's the ticket to a destination of oneness. It's a knowing and a sense of awe of the Divine nature of everything. It's the knowing that we are part of a Universal life energy that permeates every living thing. It's the knowing that we can immerse ourselves in this energy and access its grace and abundance. Spirituality is the recognition that things are not always what they appear to be, and life is a multi-faceted and complex illusion that we play in every day. Spirituality is that element of being within us that allows us to know and feel that we can transform our world from the inside-out.

In this new age of spirituality, more and more people are awakening to their spiritual potential. This potential needs to be nourished so we can continue to positively develop as a nation and planet. As the cumulative vibration of our world increases as a byproduct of the increase in vibration of its parts, we will see the systems comprised of greed and power become unsustainable and we will watch them crumble. This change in the vibration of our world also requires a change in the vibration of leadership; a vibration of leadership that is high and filled with love and gratitude for the self, as well as the good of the whole.

Love and gratitude are high vibrations. Hate and fear are low vibrations. I like to think that the game of life is all about increasing our vibration to the highest level possible before we exit our physical bodies.

When I was a Medical Technologist, I used to perform testing to measure titers of antibodies and other substances in blood. For example, to see if somebody is immune to the Rubella virus, an antibody titer is performed. If the titer is adequate, a person has an appropriate amount of antibodies in their blood to be immune to the Rubella virus, should they come in contact with it. A titer is defined by the concentration of a substance in solution or an antibody in serum (the part of the blood left after the red cells clot and are removed by spinning in a centrifuge). I like the word titer and so I have been speaking about a person's baseline titer of happiness for many years. I mentioned this in chapter three, as the baseline titer of happiness is my way of expressing that natural level of happiness that resides within an individual that is only measurable by the quality of their thoughts and exemplified by how they live. A person with a high baseline titer of happiness is a person who maintains a positive attitude, is resilient to the ups and downs of daily life and is a great person to be around because their positive outlook on life is refreshing, nice to be around and even contagious. In my travels, I have also found that kind of person to often look much younger than they are—and I have come to believe a positive outlook on life promotes a youth-filled aging process. I would also say this person vibrates at higher levels because this type of existence comes from a position of self-love.

A person with a low titer of happiness is often miserable, and if you take a moment to think, you can probably hear them moaning about something. There can obviously be a wide variety of reasons for their misery, but since there are no victims in this world, their titer is the result of what goes on in the "inside." A person with a high baseline titer of happiness may opt to avoid the person with a low titer of happiness, because the characteristic of their being does not resonate with them. It may feel uncomfortable and many will find being around an unhappy or negative person just plain exhausting. A person with a low base line titer of happiness can seem to suck the life out of people, sapping their energy and being a drain. Miserable people like to hang out with miserable people because that density is comfortable and familiar.

A great leader can never be produced from a person with a low baseline titer of happiness. When significant challenges are presented into the life of the high baseline titer person, those challenges are often perceived as opportunities. The high titer person will feel like there is a reason for this challenge and they will push themselves to learn and become an even stronger and more resilient person as a result of the challenge. Their "daily titer" (the one that manifests their thoughts and actions that are exemplified by how they act and react on a short term basis) may drop from their baseline in times of extreme challenge, sadness or loss, but it will only be temporary, for they will resume living from the higher perspective of love, since that is baked within the nature of their being. A miserable person may have some great things happen to them that catapult their "daily titer" for awhile but they will go back to their natural state of happiness or unhappiness in time. I've read about the unhappy person who wins the lottery and is so much happier for awhile but realizes in time that money can't resolve the sludge that flows through their insides, and so in time, they go back to being unhappy. I often wonder if moody people have a lower baseline titer of happiness when compared to people who are not moody. My guess would be yes, but I only have my opinion to substantiate most of this information. You'll need to check in and see if any of these thoughts and philosophies resonate with you. To me, unhappy and/or moody signifies the need for resolution of issues from the inside-out. I can say that I have never met a great leader who was moody. I have met moody people who occupied leadership positions, but I've never met a great leader who was moody. Moody people often need to be tiptoed around. A great leader needs toes that can't be stepped on—they need to be resilient, open and flexible. There may be leaders that save their moody for home, but I believe their core vibration will be effected by the moody factor to ultimately limit their leadership potential. The limitations of their leadership success would be a result of the boundaries they've placed on themselves. For that reason and others, I would encourage the moody person or leader to inquire within in an attempt to really understand what was going on inside. The vibration of leadership that I am speaking of is that vibration that makes us who we are and how we think. The vibration uniquely permeates all actions, regardless of location and time of day. A high baseline titer of happiness precipitates a high vibratory state, as self-love is the driver of that existence.

The way to increase a baseline titer of happiness is through the self-mastery journey. The scientist in me also loves the word titration, a close relative to titer. In the lab, a titration is performed by adding measured quantities of a reagent or liquid that has a known concentration to a solution with an unknown concentration such that a reaction occurs and demonstrates the quantity of the unknown by some change, like color. So we'd take a solution with an unknown concentration of a chemical and add a solution with a known amount of a substance that would react with it, to make a new compound, and we'd use an indicator like a ph change to let us know we were successful—for example, the clear liquid would turn color from clear to dark blue. As the titration proceeds, it's easy in the beginning, but the closer you get to the endpoint you desire, the more difficult the last steps become. It gets very delicate and important towards the end of the titration, as you carefully and skillfully place the known concentration of solution into the unknown, drop by drop, until the reaction occurs and the instantaneous change in color is seen. When we do the work from the inside-out, we titrate out all our wounded beliefs—our fears, our anger, our disappointment, our sadness, our grief and our anxiety –with an infusion of LOVE. The journey may start out easy but as it progresses, one needs to carefully, lovingly and skillfully tackle the deepest fears and emotions that reside in the deepest recesses of our subconscious mind and our spirit. When we have extinguished or transformed our old beliefs and emotions by removing the manifestations of fear and replacing them with love, the color and change we see is a state of bliss, a life of joy and the light of inner peace. With this personal growth and development, our baseline titer of happiness increases. Doing the work from the inside-out will resolve those deep seeded issues that prevent us from fully loving ourselves and recognizing the light that shines so brightly in our spirits. The most important shadow to recognize is the shadow that our ego creates and casts upon our lives. An outstanding leader needs outstanding self-control, most notably, self control of the ego. Remembering and recognizing the light within is a good antidote for a hyperactive ego. After all, in order to see, there must be light!

It's important for a leader to ask themselves if they like what they're doing. A leader who loves to be a leader will exude that energy and assist in the creation of a successful organization. A miserable leader will attract more of the same. A frustrated leader who is in a position that is over their head may not only have success issues but they may eventually make themselves sick. When a leadership role is desired solely for money or prestige, the vibration or energy associated with this type of leadership will eventually attract similar deceit. A leader will reap what they sow, just like everyone else on this planet.

Chapter Eight

The Stimuli of Illusions

An illusion is something that deceives the mind or senses by fooling it into believing that it exists when it doesn't. An illusion appears one way when in fact, it really exists in another or different way. It can be a false belief about oneself or other people. It can be a false belief about a situation or about anything else in life that can present as one thing but turns out to be something different. The power of the deception lies within the human mind and the lens by which we view life and develop our perceptions and conclusions about ourselves, anybody, anything and everything. The more we focus on anything the larger it becomes and remains in our view. We live in world where we tend to give life to all kinds of thoughts, perceptions, statements and events that only become real because we make them that way. The work place is no exception to the plague of illusions.

It is paramount to be honest and open with all levels of leadership and staff at all times. That level of trust is essential because it will be the foundation upon which all communication and production is built. If the staff gets a whiff of a hidden agenda or that things are different than presented by leadership, the staff will create their own version of the story and illusions will be created. These illusions will make it to the grapevine and from there the breath of life will be infused into the illusions, giving them the power to present themselves as real and become integrated into the organization as truth. Inevitably, the leadership team will subsequently need to address issues that don't exist and time and energy will be wasted on the ramifications of this drama. These ramifications include an effect on morale, productivity and finances. The misdirected or misinformed employee's mind often creates a story that is far more interesting, significantly more dramatic, way more complicated, frequently exaggerated, and most often not consistent with the truth. Great leadership requires an energy and motivation to proactively, intuitively and instinctively see and understand the possibilities for the creation of illusions within any given situation well in advance of their manifestation. A leader needs to have their finger on the pulse of the *potential* for the creation of illusions to ensure that any miscommunications or misperceptions are corrected before they are allowed to create false beliefs.

To do this, a leader needs to do their own work, from the inside-out, to evaluate their individual propensity for creating illusions and the level of drama they create, are comfortable with, and even enjoy in their lives. Some people thrive on drama. Drama can give them a sense of purpose and make them feel good or better about themselves. Drama can make people feel needed and give them a sense that they're a part of the swirl of inside information and knowledge. People in leadership positions can be the same way. If they are drama oriented, at an unconscious level, managers will believe that by creating chaos, they will be needed to help mitigate the blowback. They will feel needed and important. From a day-to-day operating standpoint, a leader should strive to be the least important person in the organization. They should foster an environment where groups are self-directed and can solve their own issues in a productive, honest, fair, consistent and loving manner. They should allow the leadership team that reports to them to feel confident to make their own decisions. They should instill a knowing that should a decision be made that doesn't align perfectly with the way the boss would do it, they'll support it just the same. If a leader can't do that, they are either hiring the wrong people or they're not cut out to be a leader.

We do not respond to stimuli but to stimuli as we interpret them. The stimuli travel through our lens of perception and understanding, spiced with all the subconscious beliefs and conclusions we've derived about ourselves and the world. This interpretation subsequently elicits a cascade of reactions in the human body. These reactions primarily occur in the nervous and endocrine systems of the body—those systems most responsible for homeostasis. Homeostasis is the body's desire and ability for balance or equilibrium. This concept of the role of the nervous and endocrine systems and our perceptions and beliefs will be further developed in chapter nine, as we continue to link our emotions to chemical reactions that occur within the body that can produce a sense of wellness or dis-ease.

The workplace is a prime environment for interpreting error and giving it power. There are many opportunities to misunderstand a person's intentions and what was at the heart of their communication and actions. By communication I'm referring to verbal, non-verbal and written. Email is an excellent medium for misunderstanding because the words lack emotion. "I need to see you to discuss an issue," can be taken in a variety of ways without the inflection of voice. Special care must be taken to put quality in email communications.

One of the most common reasons why people misunderstand people at work is because they don't really know them well enough. They may never know the personal circumstances around their growth and development and the patterns of their perceptions that drive how they speak and how they act. One of my favorite analogies is one I made up while eating my morning cereal and thinking about the workplace. My cereal box is filled with many different grains, some fruits, some nuts, and some honey clusters, all held together by the common bond of being called to be my breakfast cereal. The growth cycle of each component is unknown to me. All I'm sure of for growth to have occurred is that I know there was rain and I know there was sunshine. I don't know the origin of their source or the ratio of the two, I am only aware of the quality I see, the freshness I experience and the flavor that keeps me coming back to my cereal every morning. We hear our co-workers say things and do things that are a reflection of their beliefs. What you hear and see is a direct result of what people think of themselves. We respond to people, sometimes quickly, assimilating the data of speech and action through the filters that reflect how we feel about ourselves. Our interpretation of what occurs and what is said, the manner in which the information presents, how they said it, what they did, and how they did it becomes the justification for our response. We give ourselves credit for being able to correctly assess the information and select the correct choice of words and actions in response to what our lens of life has shown us. Our interpretation and our subsequent response may be accurate and it may be inaccurate. We tend to interpret, believe and give power to what we perceive to be true. When we make inaccurate interpretations real, we create more illusions through the power of thought. There is a genuine danger to thinking we know and understand the motives of others. We will never know what is inside anyone else. We will never understand and appreciate the magnitude, variety, pain and joy of the voluminous sights, sounds, smells, and events that somebody has lived through, from this lifetime or before (if you believe in past lives), from the womb to the cradle, from the cradle to the grave. It's common to respond to people as if they have intentionally done whatever we perceive to be true. We should not even begin to analyze the motives of others or try to fully understand the perspective they have come to embrace, because we will never have the complete and accurate data set. People don't even have the complete and accurate data set in their conscious mind because a significant portion of the complete data set is stored in an unemotional, database-like medium called the subconscious mind (more about this in chapter sixteen). The energy we place on analyzing other's motives should be spent analyzing our own motives and delving into the world of our own beliefs.

Our self-directed thoughts precipitate our myriad of emotions. Our layers of consciousness create anger, sadness, anxiety, depression, jealousy, and shame to name a few. These self-directed thoughts also create our happiness, joy and bliss. We have the power to control our thoughts and work through our emotional challenges through expression and release. We have the ability to choose happiness and inner peace. We just need a sincere desire to want to travel into our mind and soul to figure out who we are. We need to maintain a sincere desire to understand how various stimuli precipitate the reactions and emotions and feelings that rule our life. The mental gymnastics of creating our own scripts for somebody else's life happens anytime, anywhere. A leader must understand the dynamics of how people think and how inaccurate perceptions drive the same bus at work as they do any other time of the day or night.

We often stress ourselves because we perceive that "stuff" is happening to us, instead of just happening. We tend to make things about us when they're not. We personalize and scrutinize and subsequently jeopardize and sabotage our potential for a life lived in a state of joy. For a work environment to be filled with harmony, peace and accountability, the sum of its parts must add up to that matrix. The more conducive a work place is to allowing people to feel good about themselves and assisting in the building of confidence and self-esteem, while at the same time, mandating accountability for all words and actions, the more successful the organization will become.

Our internal dialog with ourselves is known as self-talk. It is our internal language of thought. Self-talk runs rampant in our heads all day long—telling us how we feel about ourselves and the world in which we live. This self-talk is the alphabet with which we create the sentences that describe and interpret our environment. Self-talk can be controlled by the power we can access through our higher self or the spiritual aspect of our being.

The workplace offers a unique opportunity to expand the spiritual aspects of ourselves because the workplace is saturated with challenge.

Being successful at work is not solely about technical skill and performance. It's about attitude and how the performance is delivered. A highly skilled but abusive, miserable and negative person will not be a healthy and productive addition to the workplace, irrespective of their intelligence. The ability to maintain a positive outlook on life and be a happy person resides in our spirituality. Our emotional and mental health is irrevocably intertwined with our spirituality because we are spiritual beings. We are spiritual beings who have decided to have a physical experience. We came to Earth to love and be loved, to hear and be heard, to see and be seen, to touch and to feel and to know—with or without eyes that see and ears that hear and hands that touch. There are many reasons why we should not ignore our working hours and think that the enrichment of our spirituality should primarily occur after work and on weekends, holidays and vacations. The workplace is an excellent venue to enhance our spirituality and it is a wise person and leader that knows and understands this concept.

When you work full time, you usually work at least 40 hours per week. There are 168 hours in a week. If you sleep 7 hours per day, that leaves 119 waking hours. That means we spend at least 34% of our waking hours at work with people who may or may not be member of our circle of trust. It is likely that the people who mean the most to us don't work with us. Although it may seem as though you're stuck working with some people, as you may believe you would have never selected them to play that role, at a soul level, I believe we put everyone who means anything to us in our path for a reason. I'm referring to both positive and negative influences. The biggest irritants in life will offer the greatest opportunity for growth for we can thank the people who drive us crazy for helping us evolve mentally, emotionally and spiritually.

There are major opportunities for misunderstandings at work. Misunderstandings offer growth in our personal and professional development. During our work day, we can be like machines working at high speed to get the job done. In our quest for speed and accuracy, we may lack attention to how we are coming off and how we are being perceived. Our preoccupation with high performance can render us unaware. We may speak or act in haste and it can be misunderstood as a lack of tolerance, being in a really bad mood, or being generally grouchy and miserable. It's important to pay attention to how we come off to other people and it's important to understand that people have bad days and we can't take things personally. When this type of situation is habitual, it is a sure sign that the person is having some sort of issue or perhaps they are not meant to do that particular job. We should always cut people slack on occasion, but both the employee and leader have to deal with this issue if it's ongoing and daily. It will be a downer for the team or workgroup and eventually you can lose good staff if they feel uncomfortable or abused.

We react to stimuli differently when we're stressed and work usually offers an abundance of opportunities to feel stress. In many, many, years past, when humans were running from the lions, tigers and bears, our bodies were adept at kicking in the fight or flight response. As blood is shunted to our extremities for speed and the big getaway, a cascade of reactions occurs in our bodies. When we're at work, and when it's very stressful, we sometimes lose our ability to think clearly, as our body is reeling from the stress because we're groping to hang on to our sanity. Aspects of our personalities are altered when we are stressed. For example, an agreeable person, when stressed to the max, may act domineering and aggressive. A person who is usually analytical, when stressed to a high level, may make irrational decisions. It's important to be aware of how we are perceived when we're stressed. It's always a good idea to take note of the tone of our voice and the tenor of our words, especially when we are stressed. The work place offers a plethora of opportunities to tweeze out the worst in our personalities. Seeing and understanding this in ourselves and others allows us to find new opportunities in our self-mastery journey.

We react differently when we're frustrated and work usually offers an abundance of opportunities to feel frustrated. We can feel frustrated with ourselves and others. The workplace offers constant change. Many people don't like change, so the workplace becomes a playground to learn how to deal with change. Change may instigate feelings of inadequacy or ignorance and a leader must proactively prepare for change with this parameter in mind. The employees must be adequately trained and their toolboxes must be filled with all the right elements to get the job done successfully.

Many of us push ourselves harder at work than any other time of the day. We should not neglect our self-mastery journey when our energy is at peak levels. If we come home exhausted every day and don't have an ounce of energy left for ourselves and our self-mastery journey, we need to reassess our priorities and the role our work plays in our life. A leader must keep an eye out for the staff members who consistently put their personal needs aside. When the well is dry, there will be no water to quench the thirst of anyone.

The work environment offers a plethora of stimuli to elicit fear and fear can be a great teacher. Just by asking ourselves what root emotion is playing in our bodies, love or fear, we can develop a great awareness of what route our thoughts feel comfortable in taking—the love route or the fear route. This is a huge opportunity for self-mastery, as fear is the greatest inhibitor of progress at every level.

Another reason why the workplace is abundant with self-mastery or spiritual growth opportunities is that a person will usually find a friend or two who can provide honest feedback regarding their actions, reactions and abreactions in workplace situations. Even if we don't work with our families and best friends, the workplace still offers opportunities for friendship, mutual admiration, trust and love. There will be some people who will bond, develop genuine friendships and love each other. There may only be one, two or a few with true loving friendships, but in a harmonious and loving work environment, people will possess a general fondness and type of love for one another and there will be assistance and support for the self-mastery journey. At some level of consciousness people know that as individuals evolve, we all evolve. We are ONE. In being one, when the collective or unity consciousness rises, we all rise. There is a genuine benefit to assisting our brothers and sisters (not literally but figuratively speaking), to reach a level of self-mastery because it is good for the whole. As we discussed in the previous chapter, this increases the vibration of the organization because of the increase in the vibration of its parts. In turn, this increases the vibration of our planet, since we make up its parts. As the vibration of our planet increases, the world becomes a better place to live. There will be more love and the abundance that already exists will be seen more clearly and will be more evenly distributed.

For all these reasons and more, we need to acknowledge and not neglect our opportunities for soul growth at work. A person and especially a leader must acknowledge that people are doing the best they can given their self mastery progress to date. A leader must also ensure that opportunities are in place for people to continue spiritual growth, even in the workplace. This is a different paradigm of days past, but I'm confident it will prove fruitful in the near future and will be essential in the distant future. This can be done by offering different forms of therapy for the mind, body and spirit in the work place. This concept will be expanded upon later in this book.

Egos play a starring role in establishing the quality of our internal dialog and self-talk. If we would take the time to write down and analyze our self-talk, we can learn a great deal about ourselves. By stepping outside of ourselves to become the wise adult observer, we can ascertain the level of health and rationality of our internal communications and that analysis can assist us in the self-mastery journey. I love the idea of journaling and I'm a proponent of writing to express our thoughts, emotions and feelings, even if it's just once in a blue moon. When I was very young, I would write letters of what I was feeling and hide them under my mattress. With time, I let my mother read every one of them, knowing that she'd help me sort out my feelings and make sense of emotions I didn't understand. My mom was my first self-mastery mentor and I'm not sure people understand the magnitude of the importance of good parenting or guardianship, as the foundation for a life of continual self-mastery is created.

When self-talk plagues us, and we seem to be losing ground with our thoughts, we can step outside ourselves and play the role of a wise adult or parent, or goddess or god. We can make a list of all the crap or shall I say statements that continue to play in our heads and ruin our days. We can take this list and step outside ourselves and become that wise, objective force to analyze each item or statement to seek the truth. Each statement can be evaluated to ascertain whether they are real or illusions—rational or irrational. Sometimes we may make statements but what we're really afraid of is something more profound. For example, let's pretend that in the workplace, a new procedure is going to be implemented and there is going to be a competency exam after. Let's also pretend that the self-talk that is running rampant is, "I know I'm going to fail that test." Now let's pretend that you're one of the star performers in the organization and there has never been a new procedure that you didn't grasp readily and perform in an exemplary fashion. The likelihood of you failing is close to nil. What is really going on inside can be the quest to be perfect. By analyzing our self-talk or statements that repeat like songs on a CD where the repeat track button is pressed, we can learn a great deal about ourselves and find avenues to further explore in our mastery journey.

There are certain aspects to life we must accept. We are not perfect and nobody expects us to be. We place unrealistic expectations on ourselves. We're also never going to please everyone all the time. Leaders, like all people, must embrace both these concepts. Even the people that love us the most will be turned off by our behavior once and awhile. Many of us seek approval and love from everyone. That's a nice goal but it is unrealistic and a leader will make poor decisions if that's their conscious or unconscious motivation. Many of us try to be perfect and often look at our internal glass as half empty, focusing on that which can improve. We should accept the fact that we're human and flawed and look at the internal glass as half full, realizing our attributes and enriching them. The habit to form would be to nurture the best parts of us to allow them to expand, thereby crowding out the habits we wish to eliminate. When we focus on the good in ourselves, that will be the aspects that are magnified, stay in view and expand.

As I mentioned previously, when I was young, my dad would always tell me to believe half of what I saw and nothing of what I heard. That was great advice as it was another way of saying, things are not always what they seem. It's an easy way to remind yourself to not get caught up in the drama of the workplace, especially when the messages you're receiving are from the few instead of the majority.

Chapter Nine

The Value of Discomfort

Discomfort is one of the greatest gifts our mind and body gives us, for it is invaluable in helping us continuously evaluate the choices we make and the paths we travel in life. From the feeling of impending danger when our hair begins to stand on end, to that gnawing feeling in the pit of our stomach, to the muscle pain in our neck, to the tightness and ache in our jaw, to the anxiety that mimics chest pain, to the gastric ulcer that forms from ongoing stress, to diarrhea, to headaches, to the pain and suffering of emotional challenges, to dis-ease, the body uses voluminous mechanisms to get our attention and let us know something is not quite what it should be in our life. There is incredible value in paying attention to the various levels of discomfort in our lives for it often parallels the alignment of our journey with our highest good.

Leaders have a responsibility to themselves and others to develop the tools to assess discomfort. Whether it is discomfort in our bodies due to some internal struggle, uncertainty or path we have chosen or the discomfort that acts as a fleeting but resonating alarm that some work related decision, path, policy or procedure is not conducive to success, discomfort speaks volumes and assists us in our daily life. It's also important for a leader to recognize discomfort in others. A leader needs to get out of their office and frequently visit the people. It is imperative that good relationships based on trust and respect are developed between and among leaders and staff at every level on the organizational chart. Discomfort among employees who care deeply and work diligently should not be ignored. An isolated instance of discomfort is much different than a trend or pattern of discomfort. The only way for a leader to really understand what's going on in an organization is to listen to the people who do the work. The team of people, however, should be the right people. Mediocrity and bad attitudes must be eliminated by an atmosphere that prompts them to self-select out or be terminated. Termination can be done with love and respect. There a couple of essential elements to ponder regarding terminations. First, there was a reason for the employment in the first place. Growth occurs at many levels and everyone who came in contact with that employee provided some purpose and everyone learned something—whether they realize it or not. Second, if we buy into the fact that there are no failures, just redirections, a termination should be viewed and accepted as a redirection. A person who can't perform or fit in or who maintains a bad attitude is not a failure. Everyone has gifts, they just need to find the right place to use them. That person is likely to find a new job that is more suitable to their vibration. A termination should be respectful and kind.

There will be times when I will feel or recognize discomfort in the body language or on the face of an outstanding employee, who is not a complainer by any stretch of the imagination. I will always ask, "Everything ok?" They will usually respond in a way that I understand the general direction of the discomfort. Sometimes I will say, "OK, just tell me, work or something else." If they reply, "Work", I will not let that die until I understand the source of their discomfort or frustration. I may not be able to do anything about it at that moment, but I will file it away to assist me in maintaining the kind of work environment I feel is conducive to a healthy, harmonious and productive work place. If they respond, "Oh—it's not work," I'll say, "Oh, well I hope you're ok, I'm always here if you need me." Some leaders may say, "I don't have time for that..." and I would respond, "Make time, for that is one of the most important roles of a good leader." In the event a work place has thousands of workers and it really is physically impossible to meet the people, I would ensure that every level of the leadership team maintained that philosophy and made the people the priority, and I would also ensure the CEO was at least familiar with everyone in leadership. This is what service based leadership is about, asking yourself not what the people can do for you, but what you can do for the people. If this brings a CEO discomfort, my next suggestion would be to dig deeply to see if leadership is aligned with their highest good and the highest good of others. Some people like to be leaders because it makes them feel good or they like the money. In the long run, for the evolution of soul, power and money are not what matters. The greatest power we have is the one within ourselves. Love and gratitude and a knowing of abundance along with hard work and diligent efforts will provide the energy and intention of economic stability and comfort.

Discomfort is an innate gift not a burden or sacrifice or duty. There is no martyrdom in possessing discomfort. Martyrdom is our human expression of a victim mentality in action.

Self-mastery cannot be fully expressed by putting forth effort to understand our minds and acknowledge the presence of our higher self, but neglecting the physical. We have chosen to come to earth with this precious vessel we call our bodies. Our bodies deserve and need attention and care. Our physical vehicle and our breath are what differentiates our realm of existence. The self-mastery journey therefore, has a physical component that mandates a general awareness and education. It is as vital to understand how our thoughts effect our emotions and feelings in our bodies and what biological and energetic functions elicit a cascade of reactions that affect our health and wellbeing.

It is common to hear somebody say, "I've been so busy burning my candle at both ends that I made myself sick." It's rare, however, to hear, "I was on the verge of getting sick when I realized what was going on and I healed myself." Why do many people readily accept we can make ourselves sick but will not accept that we have been gifted with the same innate ability to heal ourselves? Is it because we are a people who embrace suffering as an everyday part of life? Have we been programmed that sickness is an integral part of life but healing depends on whether we deserve it? Have people been programmed that healing is decided upon by an outside influence or through the will of a higher power—like God? Do we feel unworthy of possessing healing abilities? Are healing gifts only provided to saints and holy people? I suppose there are as many answers as people, but I believe we are amidst a changing tide where people are being lead to the self-discovery that healing gifts are possessed by everyone. The power and mystery that resides within our bodies provides the mechanisms for self-healing and that power is fundamentally related to our thoughts, beliefs, guiding principles and our self-confidence.

Discomfort comes in a variety of shapes, sizes and flavors; the most profound of which, can render a life altering experience or wake-up call. Our internal auditor has a plethora of options to communicate with us. When we are highly sensitive to the internal workings of our precious human machinery, we can sense nuances of discomfort before they manifest into more challenging and acute symptoms. We have the ability to tune into our internal physician and diagnose and heal. Our bodies are filled with systems that constantly monitor our health and wellbeing because that is the role they were created to play in our life.

For instance, our immune system provides an incredible symphony of neutrophils, lymphocytes, monocytes, macrophages, antibodies and other microscopic elements that travel through our bodies in an endless cycle of transport to work in harmony to heal. At an unconscious level, we heal ourselves constantly. In some instances, however, a variable is introduced that necessitates our conscious awareness but it doesn't mean that we don't have the innate tools to continue the healing process on a conscious level. Faith and confidence in oneself, in addition to an awareness and willingness to step inside our thoughts is often the key. The interrelationship between the physical and mental are inseparably intertwined. Sadness, anger, resentment, guilt, jealousy, and anxiety are just a few examples of emotional discomfort that if left to fester may diffuse into more physical symptoms. Just as it is necessary to understand the source of these emotions and feelings, it is necessary to understand how and why they play a role in our physical health. A leader who is in tune to themselves is in tune to other people for the threads of similarity, outside of the uniqueness of each individual, are many.

In addition to paying attention to our bodies from a health and wellness perspective, leaders must be aware of the discomfort tool and the incredible value that it plays in the work place and in the alignment of our soul journey as it relates to a career or day to day operations, decisions, and processes. I'll give you an example. Many years ago, I was working as the administrator of a large medical practice, the president of which was embarking on a new real estate venture that most people felt was going to be a great benefit to the community with a substantial return on investment for the company and its principles. As discussions commenced about this project, before any real planning and preparation had occurred, my intuitive feelings began to surface about the project and myself. I had an uncomfortable feeling within me, similar to an internal gnawing in the pit of my stomach but without pain. It was just discomfort. It was that familiar feeling, deep inside myself, that always alerts me to the fact that at some level of consciousness, the winds of change were in motion and I must pay attention. At this time in my career, it was the fourth time I experienced this gut feeling that told me I was getting ready to move on to my next opportunity and chapter in my career. I began to contemplate my next adventure and I was wide eyed and open to signs and signals from the Universe that have always lead me to my next position. My intention was always that I would be sent where I was needed. My desire was to be lead to a place where I could make a significant difference and contribution but also, a career move that would be within my highest good and the enrichment of my professional and personal growth. Recognition of my commitment to my family was also paramount. I could never be successful at the expense of my children. They always came first and I have been blessed that my employers never asked me to choose between my daughters and my job. They always knew they would lose anyway, since I made my priorities very clear to any prospective employer. I was never motivated by money, but to my surprise, that kept rolling in, too. As I waited for my next opportunity, I still gave my current employer everything I had to give. I think this is important—when there is another position within the company or elsewhere that a person desires to possess, focus must remain on the current position. When a person focuses on getting a promotion, it's common to lose site of the present needs of a department and expend energy is that unproductive and unnecessary. In addition, because of a lack of focus, should performance in the current position falter, it can be recognized such that when the promotion becomes available, current work performance and levels of production and excellence may indicate unsuitability for the promotion. It's an easy trap to get caught in and it's sad to miss out an opportunity because of short sightedness and focus on the future instead of the present. The objective should be to always do your best and be prepared for the next opportunity, not pretend you already have it.

As that real estate project began to take form, planning and discovery meetings commenced. Whenever I was in a meeting related to this venture, I became a bit sick to my stomach and a touch queasy. The first time I just took note of how I felt and wondered what was going on, but when the feelings recurred during every meeting about that project, I knew my higher consciousness was speaking to me. It became clear to me that this real estate venture might not be as easy or successful as my work group desired. I resigned my position shortly after the commencement of these discussions and I was thankfully not involved in the significant challenges and ramifications of that project. It was very clear to me, that should I be involved in that project, my work life would become challenging and thankless and I knew there wasn't a fraction of that project that was meant for me. I share this story because throughout my entire career, I can honestly say that there is almost always some level of discomfort from a minor nuance to a striking hit that alerts me to pending doom with a project, procedure, analysis or job. I know this sounds dramatic, but this intuitive feeling of discomfort has led me to turn away from chaos and negative outcomes and towards more successful paths in my career for over 25 years. I never neglect that feeling, and I always try to pay attention and understand what my insides and outsides are trying to tell me. This tool can be used in our personal lives as well as our work lives.

Regardless of where we sit, discomfort has meaning. It's essential for us to learn how that discomfort feedback loop works uniquely within ourselves and it is equally imperative to learn how to interpret the signals our physical, emotional, mental and spiritual bodies send to our conscious awareness.

It's also essential for a leader or anyone else, to understand that the same mechanisms are occurring in everyone else. By attempting to understand the complexities of people, a higher level of tolerance is often created. Discomfort can also be that signal to a leader that they are not paying attention to an aspect of their work. When there is something going on at work that is less than optimal, whether it is financially or operationally oriented or perhaps related to employee morale or marketing services or anything else that goes in a workplace, when I start to get feelings of discomfort, I analyze what those feelings are telling me and why I am having them. It's usually an indication that I need to pay more attention to something or somebody or a group of people that I have put on the back burner. It often means I need to get off my chair, out of my office and take time to roam around and listen to the people. To analyze our discomfort, it's helpful to understand the level of power our thoughts have on the cascade of chemical reactions in our bodies.

Homeostasis was briefly discussed in the previous chapter. That balance is a gift primarily brought to us by our nervous and endocrine systems. Science has taught us that there is a chemical to match every emotion. We know that our cells have receptor sites located within the surfaces of our cell membranes. Like the lock and key analysis of enzymes and substrates that we learned in grammar school life science and high school biology class, when a chemical circulates in our bodies that finds a corresponding cell receptor match, the chemical binds to the cell membrane. The chemical that binds to the receptor site is called an effector. When effectors bind to receptors, they come together like complementary pieces of Velcro and the result is a change in the cell. We know that receptors expand by usage. This concept and process is beautifully and clearly demonstrated in the movie, *What the Bleep Do we Know*. If you have any interest in this, I highly recommend the movie. There are companion books to the movie that are also helpful. Additional books/Audio CDs related to this topic are available from

Drs. Bruce H. Lipton and Candace Pert. Both Dr. Pert and Dr. Lipton's excellent works provide scientific data to support the mind-body-spirit connection.

The scientists in the movie, *What the Bleep Do We Know* explain how we become products of our emotions and how receptors expand by usage. This usage is likened to belief systems and our responses to anything and everything. Addictions are another outstanding example of how receptors expand by usage. The effect of stress on our bodies is another prime example of how we become products of our emotions.

The nerve cells in our bodies are highly specialized and they allow impulses to be transmitted to nerve networks and cells outside the nervous system. Impulses are connected by thoughts and memories built on the law of association. These memories are stored in this network— memories of love, rage, hurt, pain, suffering, etc. For example, whenever I smell Jean Naté, my heart opens and fills with love because that is the fragrance my mother commonly wore and I am immediately transported to my youth to a time when she was alive. That smell elicits such warm and loving feelings. Whenever I smell cut grass, however, I immediately return to the three months of my first pregnancy when the smell of cut grass made me vomit. It took me years to change the association between the smell of cut grass and feeling nauseous. After I delivered my daughter, when the raging vomit hormones were no longer circulating in my body, I still felt nauseous when I smelled cut grass. That association had been firmly established. Subsequent to a lot of talking to myself and self-discipline to change that association, after a couple of summers, I could smell cut grass without feeling nauseous, but I never regained the fondness of the smell of cut grass that I possessed prior to my pregnancy. Those two examples are deeply seeded impulses that are connected by thoughts and memories built on the law of association. Through practice, these nerve cells form long term relationships. Some associations we develop are in our best interest and others are not. The mechanism of action of the impulses that are connected by thoughts and memories built on the law of association, like our subconscious mind, does not possess any level of understanding of whether an association is good for us, bad for us or indifferent. The mechanism of action naturally and instinctively knows its role and responsibility within our bodies. A statement in the movie, *What the Bleep Do We Know,* that I love is, "Nerve cells that wire together, fire together." I hope you can see the power of thoughts come into a more clear view and I highly recommend this movie to help build that understanding.

The endocrine system secretes hormones and neurohormones that are transmitted to tissues in our body via our blood and body fluids. The hypothalamus is the organ in our brain that acts like a mini-factory that assembles the chemicals to match emotions. It assembles the chains of amino acids (peptides) to form neuropeptides and neurohormones that match emotion. These chemicals are released from the hypothalamus via the pituitary gland—there's a chemical to match every emotional experience.

Billions of receptors in our bodies receive information that brings forth a cascade of reactions in our bodies. It's amazing that each cell in our bodies is alive and conscious and can change depending on the signal of the receptor. Over time, the more surface area of the cell membrane that gets filled with these receptors the more they squeeze out others and one can extrapolate that we become products of our emotions. Most of the adults in our work place have learned to control their outside behavior and don't throw themselves down and have tantrums but many have not mastered the control of their inside behavior. A leader must be in tune to the fact that the employee's actions and attitudes represent the internal dialog that is constant. How they act will speak volumes to what is going on inside and exemplify the products that they have become as a result of their emotions. Once again, I highly recommend two authors that do an outstanding job of presenting a plethora of information related to the concepts introduced in this chapter. Both Bruce Lipton, Ph.D. and Candace Pert, Ph.D. have authored remarkable books, namely, *The Biology of Belief* and *Molecules of Emotion*, respectively. Dr. Lipton's audio CDs called, *The Wisdom of Your Cells* is also an invaluable resource.

The hypothalamus receives signals from nearly every part of the body. In times of stress, it may activate a variety of mechanisms that prepare the body for the fight or flight response. Our sympathetic nervous system (the part of our autonomic nervous system that functions involuntarily), in response to the fight or flight activation, yields a variety of impulses that cause a cascade of reactions in our body. A rise in blood glucose or sugar levels, a rise in glycerol and fatty acids, an increase in heart rate, an increase in blood pressure, an increase in the breathing rate and a dilation in our air passages are a few. In addition, the shunting of blood from our digestive system to our skeletal muscles and extremities (arms and legs for running away) occurs, as does an increase in the production of epinephrine. Concomitantly, during stressful situations, the hypothalamus is stimulated such that there is an increase in cortisol production after the involvement of the pituitary and adrenal cortex and the secretion of a hormone called ACTH (adrenocorticotropic hormone). Cortisol is involved in multiple bodily functions such as blood pressure regulation, cardiovascular function, immunologic function, and the metabolism of fats, proteins and carbohydrates. A certain amount of cortisol is needed to maintain optimal health but too much cortisol can cause health issues. Cortisol levels do not decrease as we get older, so aging is does not provide a protective mechanism. Perhaps getting wiser is the key. Most anatomy and physiology books can provide more information regarding the science of our nervous and endocrine systems.

The process of self-mastery includes a physical component, as well as a mental, emotional and spiritual component. All systems work in harmony to achieve balance, inner peace and wellbeing. A leader who promotes the self-mastery journey for themselves, as well as all the people they work with, live with and hang out with, should have a basic understanding of how our bodies respond to love, fear, stress, anxiety, jealousy, etc. Optimal health is conducive to creating a happy life. Being happy and healthy help a leader become more resilient to the pressures of life. Everyone should cherish this vehicle called our human body. It is this precious vehicle that carries our soul through this land of opportunity called earth. It is our soul that has decided to partake in this adventure using this vehicle, not the other way around. Neither component should be ignored. They should be understood, well taken care of and treasured. More work places offer employees the opportunity for exercise than in years past. Taking care of the body and helping the work force make healthy choices, always supporting the importance of disease prevention is vital to a successful organization.

Coupling the scientific evidence with information of energy systems lends further insight into our self-mastery journey. In chapter seven, I mentioned the chakras of our body. We have seven major chakras or energy centers in the body. The first chakra is called the root chakra and is located at the base of the spine. The vibration of this chakra corresponds to the color red. Each of the chakras, when open and functioning most effectively, rotate clockwise. The second chakra is called the sacral chakra and that is located between the navel and the root chakra. The vibration of this second chakra corresponds to the color orange. The third chakra is called the solar plexus and its color is yellow. The fourth chakra is the heart chakra and its color is green. The fifth chakra is located in the throat and it is the color blue. The sixth chakra is located between the eyebrows at the mind's eye, and its associated color is indigo/

violet. The seventh chakra is called the crown chakra. It is associated with white or white and gold. The chakras develop fully at different ages and energy blocks in the chakras can be associated with malfunctions in the organs associated with the chakras. I believe that it is as important to maintain balance in the chakras and our energy systems as it is to eat healthy, exercise and learn to master our minds.

About 20 years ago, somebody gave me a book about energy systems and chakras. I started reading it and thought the information was unscientific and sort of crazy. I never finished reading the book, as it was not the kind of book for me. Ten years ago, when exploring, developing and implementing an Integrative/Complementary Therapy program for our cancer patients, I needed to understand the modalities that I would begin to support and encourage. That exploration was life-altering and today, in addition to still being the CEO, I am a Reiki Master and a Certified Hypnotherapist and maintain a thriving private practice. Energy modalities continue to be more widely accepted by the medical community. Most of my clients are referred to me by our oncologists. Sometimes the time is just not right to wake up to a new idea, theory or philosophy. When that status changes, something inside will always lead us to where we need to go if we keep an open mind and always continue to seek personal growth.

All the operating systems inside our bodies combined with those on the outside, located within the auric fields of our bodies (the electromagnetic vibratory fields associated with our physical, mental, emotional and spiritual bodies that extend out from the physical body to form different layers and colors and vibratory fields) act in concert to provide a symphony of health, happiness and a state of joy and inner peace. Each system deserves attention and communicates with our body, mind and spirit in various ways. Discomfort is our personal fire alarm that every system that we have discussed has access to pull. It is never a false alarm—there is always meaning. The self-mastery journey is the "Rosetta Stone" that allows us to decipher the purpose, meaning and value of discomfort. Discomfort that is continually ignored can end up being called dis-ease.

Chapter Ten

The Drama of Life and the Co-Created Plan

Many ask themselves, "For what purpose am I here or how they heck did I get here?" "Here" can mean alive on the earth or any given situation, such as a job, a marriage, a partnership, a friendship or even a project at work. Confusion and fear related to the uncertainties, anxieties and adversities of life create drama. Humankind, through the ages has evolved and lived through voluminous technologic advances and gained a vast array of scientific knowledge. In many ways, our lives have been made much easier. From the advancement and comfort of farm equipment, to the birth of electricity, to the invention of washing machines, to the understanding and treatment of human function and disease states, to the development of numerous and sophisticated modes of transportation, to household gifts such as the microwave oven, to the speed and dexterity of communication mediums and the instant access of data and people from continent to continent, we have come a long way in our relatively short history. We've made our lives so much easier and it seems that the potential for personal gratification gets more instantaneous every day. One would think that stress levels would be reduced and happiness become an epidemic from all the advancements and new technologies. I don't see that as the case. So many are working at record speeds and still can't get all their stuff done in the hours we were given in a day. For many, their best just doesn't seem good enough and there's a trail of stress and disappointment that follows them. In this quest for technology and knowledge, perhaps the commitment to our mind and spirits has been put on the back burner? When we don't pay attention to taking care of "the whole", stress and drama find opportunities to insert themselves into our lives. Many are forgetting to take time to breathe. I don't mean breathe but b-r-e-a-t-h-e. The strength of the mind-body-spirit connection has a direct correlation on our health, our resilience and our level of immunity to drama. There has been an awaking to this importance and so many are taking action through exercise and modalities such as yoga, that connect the flow of the breath to creative and effective positioning and stretching of the body. How did our society grow so rapidly and advance so significantly that we managed to have the mind-body-spirit significance fall through the cracks for so many years? Somehow, way back when, the mind-body-spirit connection, disconnected.

When we look back on paradigm changes through the ages, one of the most notable that caused serious religious persecution was when Copernicus shared his thesis that the sun did not revolve around the earth but that the sun was actually at the center of our solar system and in fact, the earth revolved around the sun, as did the other planets. This almost resulted in Copernicus' execution and death because his theory was in opposition to the accepted teachings of the times that were also consistent with biblical writings. For similar reasons, centuries ago I believe a separation between the body and mind became necessary to allow scientific exploration to escape religious scrutiny and persecution. This split gave way for scientific, technologic and medical theories to develop and flourish. The idea that the body was something tangible and measurable, while the mind intangible and elusive was a common thought and teaching during those times. These concepts led to great progress in the sciences. Opportunities for scientists to follow their quest for the causes of disease and cures for illnesses grew. It was safer, appropriate and necessary for scientists and philosophers to disconnect the mind, body and spirit. Spiritual and soul issues fell under the auspices of the church and clergy. This disconnect also supported the philosophy that the mind did not have an effect on the body as they were separate and distinct. This theory was embraced by clergy, as well as scientists. This separation provided a safety net from religious persecution and allowed scientists to be scientists. It allowed scientists to perform their desired research and make all sorts of discoveries related to the human body, disease states and treatments that formed the basis for the theories and practice of medicine that reside today. In a way, we should be grateful for this separation because conventional medicine, healing and diagnostic modalities were given birth from this era of safe scientific and medical exploration. On the flip side, the separation fostered a more rigid atmosphere for looking inside to understand the impact of thoughts and consciousness on the world. The environment was such that science had to deny aspects of the human body that were not measurable and explainable through scientific theories. In that vein, the mind/body/spirit connection became disconnected. It's important to note that remnants of these teachings die hard, as scientific minds have been trained to accept scientifically significant and evidence based discoveries and recommendations for centuries. For example, accepting data and theories that are not studied with statistical accuracy and scientific significance falls outside most physicians' comfort zones. Many physicians feel it's most appropriate to remain neutral on integrative or alternative therapies unless published scientific data and clinical research studies support inclusion into the management of disease. In addition, we are a litigation oriented society in which physicians fall prey to so many inappropriate malpractice cases. A person can't blame a physician for taking all the precautions necessary when their reputation, medical license and personal assets can be at risk. When modalities fall outside accepted standards of treatment, an environment with a significant level of vulnerability is created. This situation can dissuade physicians from integrating alternative and/or complementary therapies into their practice. With time, however, people have embraced activities that reconnect the mind-body-spirit and healing and wellness centers are becoming more abundant. Acceptance by the medical community continues to grow and people continue to seek health care professionals that integrate holistic medicine into allopathic treatments. Centuries ago, our mind-body connection may have put it on the back burner, but its importance is gaining more momentum each day.

The importance of spirituality and the necessity of its integration into everything we think and do and feel is also gaining momentum. Spirituality or the knowing that we have the power and ability to transform our life through the innate gifts of which we were bestowed is a key element to infusing love and joy into our lives and minimizing drama. The treadmill of life revolves at such speeds that the stress of "being" has often caused us to neglect our spiritual needs. Through my years of having heart to heart talks with a voluminous number of people, it appears that people have been taught or persuaded that they are highly limited in accessing their divine self. As populations of communities, are we inundated by information and beliefs that have limited the manner in which we look at ourselves—our spiritual selves? Religious dogmas, handed down through the ages are so often accepted without thought, scrutiny or question. I'm not sure we have been encouraged to access our higher wisdom, our spiritual vision or our ability to seek answers within ourselves instead of relying on outside influences. Do you think we have been taught how to change our reality by discerning truth, thereby changing the way we think, perceive and live? Have we been taught the innate gifts we possess to heal ourselves and assist others in their healing processes?

Through all the economic growth and prosperity of our nations, there is still war, hunger and poverty. In many instances, mental health and wellbeing is sustained by self-anesthetizing. Please do not misunderstand my intention as there are states of illness and disease that absolutely necessitate the use of prescription drugs. There are also times, however, when the consumption of prescription drugs is perceived as necessary because of human behavior and common thought patterns. Some seek the silver bullet to cure whatever ails them instead of doing the work from the inside-out. This work from the inside-out is the self-mastery journey, and it is never ending and always healing. Although our planet is abundant, the feeling of lack still permeates our people. It is most tragic that the majority of generations of all people have not yet felt the necessity for peace on earth, let alone peace within themselves. Many feel inner peace is unrealistic but I believe when we remember who we are and where we came from, as related to a divine and spiritual perspective, we can move towards inner peace. There is so much chaos in our world, the manifestations of which are caused by the cumulative sum of the chaos within the hearts and minds of people. Why does the world put itself in this position? I believe to my core, that if all people really understood the interconnectedness and oneness of our existence, any lack of love, most importantly a lack of self-love, would become a tragedy of the past.

As a society, I believe many have been taught to look outside themselves to solve problems and seek guidance. Many have been fooled into thinking that only the enlightened or insane can attain inner peace. It is not often enough that people are encouraged to inquire within to seek the answers to their questions. An intercessor of some sort is often introduced in life such that people become convinced that they don't possess the worthiness or tools to show themselves the path. My experience has shown me that many are looking in the wrong places for answers. Many are convinced that they need somebody or something besides themselves and they are often made to feel guilty when they don't believe or utilize this philosophy. Our Higher Selves or our Divine Selves or our Spiritual Selves (whichever you prefer to call it), is that wise and divine part of us that is often overlooked but is always connected to the Universal life force. The more we align with our spiritual self, the more we will feel and know this connection. The stronger the connection, the less attracted we will be to human drama. Lives are complicated because of the individuals that create complications through the choices they make.

One of the most wonderful divine gifts of this Universe is *grace*. We don't need to work for it or be worthy of it—it is a gift. It sustains our ability to receive all that we need and all that we want if we will allow and accept grace into our lives. To accept anything without having to work for it a foreign concept to many and I continue to work on the energy of receiving, as it is different than the energy of creating and manifesting. The dualistic, old pattern of thought that rests deeply in many consciousnesses is that we are separate from the Divine and must be worthy and earn the right of contact and support. A gift is a gift. By definition, we don't need to do anything to receive a gift, we just need to gratefully accept it. The gift of grace allows us to receive purely by the nature of our being. Self love, self acceptance and gratitude are magnets for divine grace.

As you listen and read different forms of media, there is much fear and hysteria created on a daily basis. Drama sells, propagates itself, confuses reality, incites fear, establishes norms, drives economics and politics and wins elections. Sometimes it appears we are programmed for drama. We have nobody to blame but ourselves for complicating our lives with drama. Complicating our lives is learned behavior. How would we believe the workplace would be any different than the norm in society, since the workplace is just a sampling of the bigger picture? All the fear and drama that drives our society also fuels our workplace if it is allowed to propagate. Fear, anger and guilt occur as naturally in the workplace as it does outside of it. It takes special people to come together and work on the minimization of drama. There must first be awareness, then commitment, and then courage and confidence to seek truth, foster accountability, and put forth the effort to stomp out drama. Drama is stomped out, one person at a time, from the inside-out. It's really a commitment to the self. The reduction of drama is a byproduct of the continuous self-mastery journey. The higher the level of mastery achieved, the more non-palatable drama becomes. Drama begins to lose its grip in the life of the person who has recognized its energy drain and negative potential. When an organization is comprised of self-mastered individuals the outside or work environment will be a reflection of the inside thoughts and beliefs of its constituents and drama will be minimized. It will be replaced by understanding and a desire to work together for the good of the whole. When drama is allowed to fester in the workplace, it will spread like a contagious disease. When it's not routinely accepted and is consistently nipped in the bud by fostering accountability and self-awareness, drama will be diminished.

What makes drama and why are many addicted to it? I think, like everything else, the answer can be found when we look within and venture through the mastery journey. The human ego writes the drama, directs and produces the drama and most importantly, maintains the starring role. In the ego's need to protect itself from death, destruction, or deterioration, drama becomes one of the fundamental byproducts of its density. An aspect of the self in need of rehabilitation creates drama to sustain those beliefs held about the self. Fear is one of the greatest fuels for drama. When somebody has a self image that they are not worthy of love, they will create drama that will sustain that belief. They will prove to themselves, time and time again, that they are not worthy of love. They will attract people and situations that resonate with that same energy and they will find themselves in patterns that recur over and over in a life theme. Drama is also the result of a need to make ourselves feel needed and wanted. The victim oscillates between "it can't be my fault, it's always somebody or something else" and "I am here to save the day," and when none of those circumstances can be met for whatever reason (such as nobody is willing to sit on that teeter totter with them), victims can turn into angry people who treat others poorly. When I think of a victim mentality I think of the song my girls and I would sing when they were tots, "Nobody likes me, everybody hates me, I think I'll go eat worms, long thin slimy ones, big fat juicy ones, itsy, bitsy, fuzzy, wuzzy worms!" And like the song continues, down goes the first one, down goes the second one . . . and after time, when this cycle becomes paved in the highway of neurons, people get into a cycle of believing that they are not good enough and nothing can change that fact, as it's proven to them over and over again. Irrespective of how awesome we are, being liked all the time is an irrational desire. Even the people who adore us can get a bit sick of us now and then. When we consistently seek approval or love, we end up disappointed and angry. When we're disappointed and angry there can also be guilt or shame. Guilt or shame can be invisible masks that the drama lover wears in an effort to work out their inner dysfunctions. That will prove fruitless, as the work must be done from the inside-out. Bringing others into drama to make a person feel less guilty is ineffective.

The first step in breaking cycles of drama is to be aware of the patterns of drama and subsequently try to understand the origin or source of these internal beliefs that create and foster the patterns. It's helpful to explore the core beliefs or irrational conclusions about the self that are precipitating these patterns. In chapter 16, we will explore levels of consciousness to discover the role of the subconscious mind in the formation of the program code that rests at the base of our choices of thought. Sometimes this journey necessitates somebody to help us—perhaps a professional who can objectively assist us in uncovering deeply held beliefs that surface to create our thoughts and actions.

Our trials and tribulations of life—all the bitter pills that we must swallow, go down the hatch in a totally different way when we realize we are the authors of our life plan. It is my belief that a life plan is authored by the self, in conjunction with and supported by, the Divine consciousness of which everything and everyone is comprised. Some would refer to this consciousness as God. A co-created plan is the only way a true and loving partnership between an individual and their Source/ Universal Consciousness/God/Divine Network, etc. makes sense to me. A true partnership based in truth and unconditional love that lives in a realm of free will or free choice can only exist through mutual agreements. I believe that this Divine Consciousness, the energy of which we were created and exist, is our commonality and is the basis for our oneness. I believe we are all created from this source of unity energy. Our earthly trip was planned to assist us in a conscious way, to return to that perfect oneness. We develop and implement a life plan filled with opportunities to fulfill our objectives. Opportunities come in the form of challenges and celebrations and can be felt through discomfort and elation. This symphony of opportunity is orchestrated by the ego and the higher self. The ego is comprised by the sections called the conscious and subconscious minds.

This co-created plan becomes a quilt made of all kinds of shapes, sizes, colors and dimensions of patchwork between and among many kindred spirits and soul brothers and sisters. It is important that we understand and know at our core, that we are the authors of our life plan, the development of which is coordinated and co-created. This journey allows us to find our way back home to our original connection. The key is to awaken to that knowing and know that we are precious and divine. There is no coincidence or lack of planning that occurs when we meet people, work with people, live with people, etc. We will learn a great deal from those we love and those who love us, support us, and mentor us. As I have mentioned several times in this book, some of our greatest personal and professional growth will occur from the irritants we have mutually agreed to place in our path. When a person considers the co-created plan and the bigger picture, the statement, "things are not always what they appear to be" is underscored.

Everything is exactly as it should be and everyone is at the point of spiritual evolution that they should be, too. Nothing is good or bad, it just is. When we understand perfection is in all that we see as good, bad, beautiful and ugly, we understand that all circumstances in life are meant to assist us in our unique and individual process of evolution and self-discovery. We can subsequently explore life with acceptance, curiosity, tolerance, and love. This depth of realization and love will lead to a life filled with joy. It is a way to feel peace among the chaos. I have a print in my office, the text of which was written by "unknown" and it goes like this, "Peace—it does not mean to be in a place where there is no noise, trouble or hard work. It means to be in the midst of those things and still be calm in your heart."

Since we're human, our egos often convince us that we should be angry or stressed or worried or sad or lonely or jealous or frustrated or whatever. We must cut ourselves some slack and give ourselves the time and opportunities to accept and honor our co-created plan and the co-created plans of others. As we grow to trust and honor ourselves, we allow the all loving and forgiving parts of ourselves to more frequently function on autopilot, where we are able to realign for our highest good.

We have no one to blame for anything. If we were going to place blame, it would have to be with ourselves. I think blame is an unattractive word that signals a lack of love. As you look around you, what you see are illusions that have been packaged in a human framework, created by the sum total of the life plans that have gone before us and affect the lives we currently live. There are paradigms that we hold sacred and true, just because. As our subtle spiritual revolution continues to evolve on this planet, more and more people will be seeking peace and freedom. They will recognize that the peace they crave can be attained by using the tools located inside the self. Our spiritual evolution does not take a hiatus when we're at work. Personal, transformative evolution continues around the clock and leaders in the new millennium must understand this to foster work environments that hold accountability, self-discovery, and self-growth in the highest regard. This will allow the workplace to thrive from so many perspectives. A leader must also be aware that even when the level of drama is under control, it will have spikes that necessitate continual attention and monitoring.

We seed our lifetimes with experiences, cellular memory, karma and people that will allow for our continued growth and spiritual development. We resolve karmic obligations. We bring cell memory into each lifetime, possessing gifts that may have been perfected in other lifetimes. This helps to explain the four year old violin prodigy that amazes the world with their talent and abilities. We co-create our life with the necessity and opportunity to resolve challenges deep inside that need additional attention. Spiritual evolution expands in one direction and that's to a more evolved state of being or higher state of vibration. Regardless of what we think at any given time when we deal with the challenges of life and we perceive that we take one step forward and ten steps back, we don't. A person may say, "I've jumped that hurdle before, why is it rearing its ugly head again?" What we are experiencing is the resolution of those challenges at deeper levels because of our personal growth and enhanced ability to get closer to the core of the issue. As we evolve we can dive deeper into the resolution of old issues and heal layer by layer. When an old issue presents again, it's because there is a higher level of knowing and wisdom to resolve and eventually eliminate it. It's actually cause for celebration not depression. The increments of growth depend on our ability to overcome obstacles and challenges through self-love and self-discovery.

When our feet hit the floor in the morning, we can look at life through the lens of potential and opportunity or through the lens of limitation. It totally depends on our human free will or free choice and the view we decide to employ while living. We are the only people who limit ourselves, as we are only limited by the boundaries we place on ourselves. Each twist or turn is completely dependent upon the thoughts and actions that drive our lives. We can work from the position of knowing our potential or creating our limitations. It is worth the time to contemplate which of the two motivate life. There are many opportunities and challenges that we have chosen to place before us. Within our life plan are people, places, events and things that show up because they are in alignment with our highest spiritual evolution and our greatest good. Our workday is neither excluded from this plan nor from the challenges and opportunities for spiritual/soul growth. A leader who recognizes their divinity and realizes the existence of the greater plan not only has a responsibility to support others' journeys but they also have a magnitude of resources at their disposal to assist them. It is everyone's mission to remember their Divinity, and it is no coincidence that some people are placed in positions on this earth to assist others. We would never develop a plan without providing the tools and resources to be successful. We work with many souls for the purpose of individual and united evolution that will ultimately allow our beautiful and abundant planet to rise to the occasion and vibrate at a higher frequency, too.

As we begin our earthy adventure and engage our life plan, one of our first decisions is exemplified by our selection of our parents and siblings. They will be the first teachers that foster the level of spiritual evolution we desire and we will play the same role in their lives. There are many who have tumultuous relationships with their parents and families. Some, if asked, would say they would *never* have picked them as parents or family members if they had a choice, however, they did. Once again, things are not always what they appear to be. Some parents are abusive and one may ask, why would a soul ever decide to be born to them? Some parents die at an early age and leave their children parentless, why would anybody want to put that in their plan? Some parents are horrible role models for their children, why would anybody want that in their plan? Some parents murder their children, how could anybody put that in their plan? The answer to all of these questions, including the answer to why children select to be born to wealthy, impoverished, wonderful, rotten, divorced, non-divorced parents is exactly the same. The answer is to accelerate their spiritual evolution and/or the evolution of other people in their lives, communities and perhaps the world. Sometimes, highly evolved souls come to earth to partake in a world or community known tragedy for the primary purpose of raising the level of vibration, consciousness and spiritual evolution of the rest of us. Did not the tragedy of September 11th make all Americans and people around the world take pause? Can you recall where you were when you heard of that tragedy? Did it make you more compassionate to our freedom and the sacrifices of others? Did it make you stop and love? The lives of those people who signed on to raise the vibration of our world through their sacrifice and unconditional love were not in vain. They have earned great honor on earth and elsewhere.

I always feel that when tragedy strikes the first thoughts should be of incredible gratitude to those souls and the Divine Infrastructure that assisted and welcomed them into the realm of love and light, allowing us the opportunity to further love and evolve. This type of spiritual evolution doesn't always feel good to our human bodies or egos. It is heartbreaking and it's often close to impossible for those left behind to continue to live. I am confident, however, that we are not involved with that level of pain and discomfort without our permission. That permission may rest in a dimension of consciousness that we are yet unable to access. That is one of the reasons why things are not always what they appear to be, as what meets the eye can very much not be what really is. We can't begin to guess the history of someone's soul or the purpose of life's incidents or the desire and manner put forth to accelerate evolution. That is why judgment of others is not in our life's job description. It's hard enough fathoming, exploring, understanding and accelerating our own journey. One aspect of the co-created plan I don't think many will argue is the fact that it is rarely painless. There is often great sorrow, disappointment, anger, resentment and pain expressed as we evolve and transcend through the levels of growth.

As we live our life's plan, in an effort to nudge our consciousness for our greater good, we place speed bumps and celebrations in our path to serve to guide us to accomplish our goals. Sometimes we put boulders in our path. Sometimes the things we have done to ourselves just plain stink. When I meet loving people who are struggling so deeply—whether it is financial, health, personal or professional issues—I can't help but wonder why they'd put such challenges in their plans, but I know my role is to just love and support and believe that they, like myself, are here to grow and remember. What looks one way as we live our lives on this planet as humans is only part of the story and only explains the dimension we can see, touch, hear, feel and smell. Our role is better defined as a loving part of the whole that offers compassion and honors everyone's co-created plan. It is not always easy to honor a co-created plan, especially when we love someone and are so upset and hurt by a situation. The most difficult can be to support sickness and death, because it's so painful to watch and walk the journey with somebody we love. The pain of loss can seem overwhelming and presents as one of our greatest earthly challenges. The thought that we have "lost" someone we love is overwhelming unless we take solace by trying to understand the bigger picture. It's not always easy to honor our own co-created plan, either. It is during trying times that we must lean on a Divine Network and our families, friends and communities to provide an infrastructure of love and strength. The workplace is no exception. There must be compassion and assistance when an employee gets to the part of their own plan or the plan of someone close to them that appears catastrophic. We can provide the love to wipe tears and sooth sadness to help others find the courage to accept, love and continue the journey. It is in overcoming challenges in times of adversity that we evolve the most. It is not easy to honor co-created plans, but this is one of the greatest opportunities we have on earth to learn and live unconditional love.

When we realize that everything is in accordance with our co-created plan and that everything is in accordance with others' co-created plans as well, we become more acutely aware that there are no victims in this world. There are so many people walking the earth thinking that they're victims of something or someone and they are functioning and suffering from that victim mentality—victims of love, hate, jealousy, poverty, wealth, sovereignty, slavery, sickness, grief and more. We all find ourselves in the victim mode at some point or many points during our lives. For many, this is the starring role that consumes existence. Know that no one is a victim. We are the product of our choices from levels of consciousness, subconsciousness and superconsciousness. We are a product of the choices we made before our earthly entry and we are the product of the choices we've made every day of our lives thus far. The good news is that by changing our perspective and acknowledging the existence of our co-created plan, we can truly understand that there IS a reason for EVERYTHING.

We can't change the past but we can change the future. We continually co-create our lives. We are in control of our thoughts and emotions and we make choices every moment of the day. We can accept all the adversities in our life thus far as opportunities for spiritual, personal and professional growth and we can move on with a heightened awareness of life. Nobody gets through their childhood unscathed. We all have subconscious beliefs that were created by conclusions formed at a young age before we had the tools and wisdom to understand that many of these conclusions were irrational or unfounded. We can do many things to travel inside ourselves to understand why and how, but the opportunity for tomorrow is wrapped in choices of our thoughts of today. We can make a conscious effort to see the more global existence of our spirit and seek that bliss that is felt when one is at peace with themselves and loves who they are—faults and everything. If we can just realize that when we do our best, our best is good enough.

A leader who understands the co-created plan can also see the privilege they have in serving in a position of leadership. When one considers the divine nature of things, they see the world in a more profound way and that poignancy begins to drive the perceptions and choices of their life. A leader must be attentive to their spiritual evolution as it relates to this earthly leadership opportunity and the role they have been assigned to assist others in their journey. In all of my leadership experience, there have been many times when I have known that an employee or leader who worked with me for a brief time, did so for a purpose that transcended earthly reasons. Sometimes that brief time was joyous and other times painful. Regardless of the state of emotions or feelings, there were always reasons and I have been blessed to understand that those reasons defied gravity.

In the workplace, people come and go and it's easy to miss the value of the encounter. A leader should always look beyond the obvious.

Chapter Eleven

Introducing the 8 ½ x 11— an effective way to raise the consciousness

In May of 2002, I embarked on a new chapter of my career as the CEO of Hematology-Oncology Associates of Central New York (HOA). This practice is the largest and most prestigious and comprehensive privately owned cancer practice in the region. As I write this book, it is comprised of 16 physicians and about 240 employees. The practice has an incredible reputation for excellence and has won numerous awards for such. This reputation originated with the outstanding physicians who established the practice and has continued with all physicians who have joined the family of Medical and Radiation Oncologists and Hematologists.

When I arrived, the practice operated efficiently and had implemented many strategic initiatives that could carry it successfully into the future. The employees were bright, skilled and devoted to patient care. There had been some tumultuous turnover prior to my arrival and when I started my new job, I spent most of my time listening. I recognized the practice and employees were ready to move on and heal from the past.

I had a month off between this job and my previous position as a VP of two local hospitals, and I too, was in a good place to move on and heal from the exposure to one hospital's bankruptcy and the management and operational nightmare that ensued subsequent to significant financial challenges. During that time off, I contemplated my new role with the Hem-Onc group and meditated on what I could bring to that practice. Actually, I didn't understand meditation at that time and I didn't know that I was doing it—I thought meditation only occurred when your mind stopped and no thoughts entered while your legs were wrapped around the back of your neck!

The familiar voice that always speaks to me was as evident and clear as ever. I kept hearing the words, "Self-Mastery . . . Self-Mastery . . . Self-Mastery." At first, I wasn't sure what that meant, but as the months and years progressed, I became very sure that this message would be one that I'd share with anybody who would listen, for the rest of my life. I am as equally committed to my own self-mastery journey as I am in sharing the message of self-mastery to those ears that are interested in listening and have the ability to hear. The Universe has a way of sending people to where they can make a difference. At some level of consciousness, people have a way of seeking those individuals that can assist them in whatever journey they desire, self-mastery included.

The staff was and still is, incredible. They are compassionate and sensitive to human frailty. Their vocation is working with cancer patients. Amidst the fear and suffering is great love and hope. When I got to HOA I knew I was in the right place. My interesting and unique career path became very clear to me and all the zigs and zags and choices I made seemed to migrate into clear view. This position necessitated all the experience I had accumulated over the years, including my start as a Medical Technologist. This new position was in total alignment with my soul journey as I could feel the correctness to the core of my being. With time, using an acceptable language, it was also a good environment to introduce my ideas about self-mastery, co-created plans, egos, higher selves, levels of consciousness, and love in the workplace.

The patients continue to teach us more about life and living than anything else. Miracles happen every day where I work. Even when I don't know their names or faces, I love our patients. We all love our patients, whether we are direct caregivers or not—for the gift that they offer to our world is priceless.

Amidst these wonderful physicians and employees, I began to focus on all the usual operational parameters demanded of a CEO. After a few months, with the help of a few key individuals, I began to focus on those aspects of *being* that were heretofore only mentioned in places of meditation and contemplation, self-help books, therapist's offices, and some places of worship. I began speaking about the self-mastery journey or the trip inside ourselves to seek, understand, and remember the resources of true wisdom and love that reside within. My motto is building the team, one person at a time, from the inside-out. This was no ordinary CEO opportunity; this was a chance of a lifetime. I was made for this position in this practice and vice versa.

There is such respect for the life-altering journeys we are allowed to share. It is a privilege to work with cancer patients and the level of compassion and hope we all hold for each patient cannot falter. It requires a great deal of energy to accomplish all the day to day tasks of caring for this population of patients. Healthcare is inundated with paperwork and minutia. At the same time, the relationships we develop and the exchange of love that occurs allows our patients to penetrate our hearts and set up a vulnerability to emotions that are not usually experienced at work. It's one of the greatest gifts and challenges. I often stand in the background and watch employees give everything they can give to our patients and they do it every day. It's so important for the employees to take care of themselves and stay balanced. At some level of consciousness, we all recognize this need, but we don't always remember or have time to do it. For this reason and others, I think the 8 ½ x 11 was accepted.

In September of 2002, I began a tradition at every monthly staff meeting that continues today, almost 10 years later. Prior to the meeting, I intuitively pick-up a word or phrase that I present to the group to provoke thought, self-awareness and self-mastery. These words are divinely inspired and often correspond to the needs of our collective consciousness. What I mean is that they come from a place of spirit and they are always relevant to some people. I often get feedback from staff as to how much the presentation "hit home" for them. Even if the words are only heard by some, I know they are important. Today these presentations are in a PowerPoint format, but when I first started them I wrote the word on a sheet of paper, hence the name, 8½ x 11. These 8½ x 11 presentations are common in our practice now. I'm sure the new hires who attend the staff meetings wonder, "What?"

And so, these 8½ x 11 presentations have assisted in building a new culture for our practice—a culture of self-evaluation, accountability and love in the workplace. Whether there is awareness or not, they have raised the level of consciousness in the practice. They have often provided a spotlight to illuminate fear and drama in life and the workplace. One of our strategic initiatives in 2009 that began in June of that year was, "Drama Free by September Three." There wasn't anything special about September 3rd except that it rhymed with free and it's when summer ends, the kids go back to school and less vacations occur. It's that time of year in Central New York when most feel the party is over and it's time to kick into full speed.

My dear friend and colleague, Mary Schechter, Founder and President of the Intuitive Organization, and I have a radio show on www.

co-creatornetwork.com. It's a weekly show, called "Leaders of Light." We started this adventure in the fall of 2010 by featuring a word of the week. It was our "WOW" factor. These words came from my stock of 8½ x 11 presentations. When Mary was working with our leadership and workgroups, assisting to build the team from the inside-out, she received enough feedback about the 8½ x 11s to feel they had an impact on the work environment. Mary is a very gifted leadership coach, personal transformationalist and organizational development consultant. I highly recommend her and you can find her at www.theintuitiveorganization.com. About three or four years ago she began to work with our leadership to develop their skills and further assist them in leadership mastery. The seeds had been sown, watered and nurtured, and the time was right for an outside party to raise the bar to a higher level. The results have been profound. As a result of her work with our practice, she became extremely familiar with my 8½ x 11s because people referred to them, recalled them, valued them and she witnessed their subtle but transforming gift. I feel that I'm merely the conduit for these words of wisdom and I'm grateful for the inspiration that comes my way.

The 8½ x 11 concepts are very simple—simple but not always easy to implement because life and our egos get in the way. Unconditional love in action is not easy although it sounds lovely and attainable. As humans, we tend to put conditions and expectations on people. We need to lose those conditions and expectations and know that in the oneness, all is perfect. It may not feel, look, or smell perfect, but it is. That's the divine journey to oneness and inner peace.

You will find some of my favorite 8½ x 11s at the end of this book. They are an effective tool to raise the consciousness of the workplace but they are only one example of such. A leader needs to be creative and find ways to foster self-mastery and develop opportunities to utilize the collective consciousness of the workforce. If the workforce is not ready, the concepts can be introduced in a subtle way with a language that will be accepted. Intuition will be key to knowing what direction to proceed.

I use our staff meetings for another interesting kind of assistance. This may sound strange but I always say that someday, it will be commonplace for leaders to use the collective energies and consciousness of the team to help them manifest a desired outcome. It only works when the desired outcome is in the best interest of the whole. When I need a bolus of energy to manifest an outcome, I call upon our leaders and staff. I have taken time at our staff meetings to articulate a need and ask for their assistance, using the power of their minds, to create and manifest an outcome. I'll explain what our practice needs and I'll ask them to go home, focus on it, picture it like it's a done deal and believe that we have the power to pull it off. It works! Some may think I'm nuts, but for the most part, our organization and team members accept the possibilities. When I ask for their help, it's always because we want to create something that will be good for our entire practice, our patients and our community. Healthcare gets more challenging with each passing day. Cancer care has been hit hard with significant reimbursement cuts. Our team is dedicated to continue to provide the level of care we feel is appropriate and maintain a whole array of value added services that are only paid for by the margins produced by other services. Everyone in the organization wants us to be able to weather the healthcare storms and it doesn't cost anything for us to unite our thoughts and our hearts to imagine a successful practice. We all want our organization to be profitable enough to do kind of work we desire with the number of people to get the job done correctly and without undue stress on the systems. It gets more difficult every day but together if anybody can do it, we can!

In corporate America, many talk the talk but can't walk the talk. The only way a workforce will acknowledge the possibilities of the self-mastery journey is to see it in action. The CEO, the senior or executive leadership, and all levels of leadership must commit to live and exemplify their quest for self-mastery if they're going to expect it from others. This means integrity, positive thinking and positive attracting, being fair and equitable at all times, fostering accountability, working towards drama-free, and most of all, maintaining a consistent "good of the whole" philosophy. At the same time, the leader must continue working on clearing the clutter that resides in their mind and is reflected in all that they do and say. Kindness, love and accountability need to be a priority at all times. A leader has the privilege to control the employment status of the people who report to them. This is not a gift to be taken lightly. When we think at a soul level and understand the value of co-created plans, we tend to view disciplinary and counseling sessions a touch differently. There can be many reasons for the feelings, emotions and perceptions that envelop work relationships. The commitment to the type of love in the work place of which I speak, does not infer or suggest that mediocrity or poor performance should ever be accepted or tolerated. What it does mean is that the level of challenge for all parties has value and a purpose. Growth is often packaged in unpleasant ways. When we know that we have provided the tools necessary for an employee to be successful and we've ensured that they understand their job responsibilities, expectations, global goals and objectives, and we've exhausted the potential for correction, termination becomes necessary. When terminations are performed with love, fairness and integrity, the value of this experience has a greater potential to be understood. If an understanding and acceptance doesn't occur during this earth lifetime, it will occur at some point, at some level of consciousness or realm of existence in the future. The important parameter to focus upon is our intentions, for that is what will be recorded in the data fields of existence.

A great leader must earn a level of respect from their colleagues and workforce to be able to share the message of self-mastery in a credible and believable manner. Their life needs to exemplify what they preach. They must continue to do the work on the inside to transform themselves into the person they would like to become. They cannot ask someone to do anything they are not willing to do themselves. The leader must be creative enough to develop a methodology to convey their message in a manner that will be embraced and supported. One can say that the only reason my 8 ½ x 11s worked in our environment is because of the type of medical practice, patient acuity level, and successful financial foundations that allow us to operate successfully. This may be true but I hope in time, all organizations will be filled with people who want have the opportunity to know themselves. I witness more and more individuals searching for that spiritual meaning in their life, feeling and believing that there must be more to this challenging and sometimes quite disappointing existence.

People have a need to love and be loved. Most wake up in the morning and want to do a good job. They want to see the potential in their lives instead of their limitations. Some need a spark of motivation to see themselves in the loving light of which our Universal life force views them and supports them. People placed in a position of leadership are not there by accident. This privilege allows them to be a conduit of change and a force of love in the workplace.

Chapter Twelve

The Personality
of an Organization

Just like people, organizations have personalities, too. Some organization's personalities are compassionate and dedicated to complete quality and customer satisfaction. They are committed to the local and national economy and utilize honest, evolved leadership and people principles. They ensure the efficiency necessary to maintain profits that will sustain the mission and allow continued reinvestment in itself. Some organization's personalities are devious and are fundamentally dedicated solely to profit. This profit has the potential to be generated at the expense of the employees and is void of integrity. Whether an organization provides a good, great or terrible environment in which to work, their reputation will become well known and travel the community grape vine quite successfully. There is a myriad of corporate personalities out there but the most important message is that they possess a personality. A leader needs to deeply understand this and assist in the creation of the type of personality the owners and stakeholders desire. The personality creates the reputation and the reputation feeds the personality. Reputation becomes the basis of employee recruitment as personality becomes the basis of employee retention. Money is a great incentive but the energy and consciousness of how that money is generated and distributed will attract employees that harmonize or resonate to that energy or dominant thought complex. As our world continues to spiritually evolve, corporate patterns of greed and dishonesty will be unsustainable. We have seen the collapse of numerous organizations, business models and corporate infrastructures. As our world continues to spiritually evolve, leaders who possess the old style leadership patterns of control, greed, fear, and abuse will also sunset.

We have spent a great deal of time in this book on the importance of the self-mastery journey in life and in the workplace. We have discussed the new paradigm of leadership for our future. As with anything, however, new wisdom does not displace conventional knowledge that has proven effective through the years, it augments that knowledge and wisdom. There are sound principles of leadership that must be maintained in a loved based spiritual leadership paradigm. Operational indices that ensure a successful future of sustainability remain paramount.

Personnel make up the largest component of wages and close attention must be paid to creating more efficient systems in lieu of growing the workforce to address operational issues. When the number of tasks exceed the capabilities of the workforce, it is human nature to want to add people, especially when everyone is already stressed and it appears that time is not available for genuine and sometimes painful process improvement. Just adding people without process change will only yield larger, more inefficient work systems. It's one issue when tasks become more voluminous because volume and revenue are precipitating such, but it's another when duplication of effort, work-arounds and inefficiencies drive the magnitude of tasks. An excess in the ratio of tasks to the number of people to do the jobs may or may not increase profit but it will almost always stress out a work group, foster feelings of a lack of appreciation, generate increased turnover and in the long run be more of a liability than an asset. It costs a great deal to replace a highly skilled and trained worker. In a busy, stressful environment it is human nature to want to add people to reduce the burden of tasks and lessen stress. It often appears a more favorable alternative to reengineering processes and recreating systems. Leadership and consultants around the world have focused on this for decades and have developed all sorts of efficiency and quality indicator models and programs. My purpose is not to review these programs but to underscore the importance of efficiency and process evaluation and improvement. Cost containment measures have been implemented across every sector of our economy and many industries have outsourced jobs to other countries where the employee wages, taxes and benefits are significantly reduced. This is a sad situation for our nation.

Our healthcare industry is a mess and I have lived the challenges of this mess for over 30 years. I have also been able to flourish in this healthcare mess and my personal and professional growth has catapulted by living through these challenges. I have loved every job I ever had! I have always loved being an agent of change and I have been blessed to be able to be an agent of change with love and integrity. I can honestly say I've never compromised my integrity in any position I have ever held. Maybe it's because I've been a part of a service industry that strives for excellence and healing and has great compassion for people. There are a myriad of reasons for our state of healthcare, not the least of which is our *state of health*. Many American's state of health, wellness and prevention leave a lot to be desired. There's a good reason why idioms such as Ben Franklin's "an ounce of prevention is worth a pound of cure" still has meaning after almost 300 years. The data demonstrates that the United States' share of gross national product attributed to healthcare is the largest on the planet, but the quality of life and outcomes of health and wellness are far less than many other countries that spend fewer dollars. Healthcare reform can't occur without people taking accountability for their thoughts and actions. These actions include how we treasure our bodies and feed and nurture them. The self-mastery journey, if travelled with sincerity, would greatly assist in this endeavor to make our nation and the world a healthier and more peaceful and vibrant place to live. As the self-mastery journey progresses, relationships with food and physical fitness are altered. As we love our bodies more and begin to resonate with healthy thoughts and healthy living, our relationship with food and fitness naturally progresses to states of better health, wellness and prevention.

The personality of an organization is related to and affected by the mission, values and guiding principles. Every organization should have a mission statement. The statement should be easy to understand and remember. It shouldn't be so long that people's minds have an opportunity to wander or they get tired while reading it. It should have meaning and resonate in the minds and hearts of all employees. For example, our mission statement at Hematology-Oncology Associates of CNY is: *to provide the highest level of quality care in a healing environment for mind, body and spirit of patients dealing with cancer and blood disorders.* I love that mission statement. It has such profound meaning and implications for all employees. The story of how this mission statement came about is interesting—or at least I hope you'll find it that way.

The story starts when I was one of the VPs of two newly affiliated hospitals. Each set of leadership from the individual hospitals came together for a one-day retreat in a lovely and nature filled venue. One of the many purposes of this retreat was to develop an updated mission statement. I recall my first surprise at this retreat was the new VP of Human Resources that I was unaware was hired. I remember thinking that better communication should be among the leadership objectives to discuss. In any event, we spent hours talking about the mission statement. I remember how passionate I felt that healing should be among the words in the mission statement and I recall explaining the various definitions and connotations of the word healing. Being my usual self, there was a bit more *touchy feely* suggestions made. Most humored me because I had wonderful relationships with them and they respected the work I did. I didn't mind that the updated mission statement didn't include any of my suggestions. I wasn't surprised and I was actually very happy and satisfied with the updated version. I can't recall one word of that mission statement but I know I was pleased when it was complete. What I didn't know is that I was really spending a great deal of time writing the mission statement for the next corporation of which I would soon become the CEO. I was really contemplating the aspects of a mission statement I felt could reach out to employees and patients. Things are not always what they appear and in time, I was so thankful that none of my suggestions were taken when that mission statement was updated, so the words would be available when I needed them.

About 18 months later, the leadership of Hematology-Oncology Associates and I were preparing for the open house for our new 65,000 square foot cancer center. It was and still is a beautiful and comprehensive cancer center that provides all services under one roof. One hour before the guests were to arrive, I thought it would be nice to print and frame our mission statement to place on each floor of the building for all to see. When I read the mission statement, however, it did not resonate with what we did, how we did it, and what I believed we all felt while serving our patients. I sat down at my computer and literally, within a few minutes, I wrote our current mission statement. After I completed it, I had a chill from my head to toes when I read it, and I knew I must have had tapped into some Divine assistance. I raced out of my office so I could have the physicians and our leadership team read and respond to the updated mission statement. I excitedly watched their reactions and went back to my office to print, frame and distribute the new version. Years later, it's not uncommon for me to hear wonderful comments about our mission statement from patients and employees. It is displayed throughout our offices. I am grateful for that one-day retreat with the colleagues from my previous place of employment where I contemplated the value, meaning and purpose of a mission statement for hours. It prepared me for the less than five minutes I would have many months later to connect to those thoughts and the divine inspiration available to everyone—such synchronicity. The orchestration of events is never a coincidence to me.

In addition to a mission statement, many leaders and organizations find it advantageous to develop a vision statement, core values and guiding principles. Although the situation presented itself for me to have to write the mission statement by myself, I merely put words to what everyone already lived in our organization. I believe it's always best to develop these statements, values or principles using the combined gifts and collaborative efforts of all leadership. I think of a vision statement as the words that inspire an image that corresponds to the mission statement. The vision statement should represent what an organization is trying to achieve. It gives substance to the mission statement as an added statement that can inspire clarity with all employees to further express what you're trying to accomplish.

Core values are words or phrases that articulate the characteristics that are expected to be utilized and revered by all employees. They should also be simple to understand. Developing our core values was actually a fun process and was accomplished by all leadership in our organization. Our core values are *honesty, compassion, accountability, respect, responsibility and quality.* They are simple words that speak volumes. As with many other aspects of life simple does not mean easy. When core values are developed in an organization, they should be rolled out to all employees and new hires. An easy way for employees to be reminded of the mission and core values is to have them printed on the backs of their ID cards. Presenting and reminding employees about an organization's core values provide a nice entry to a higher level discussion about the fundamental characteristics of people that should drive the thoughts, emotions, feelings and actions of all employees.

A guiding principle is relatively self-explanatory. I often wonder if the guiding principles that foster activity in many corporations are honestly contemplated. I think every organization's guiding principle could be the same—*every effort will be made to make decisions that are in the best interest of the whole.* If every organization made this their guiding principle, I wonder what kind of a world would be created. We can still be a capitalist nation and be dedicated to the good of the whole. So many Americans were sickened by the huge bonuses that were provided to Wall Street executives and their employees after the economic bailout. I'll readily admit I'm no expert economist, but the validity and honesty of reported information remains questionable to me. Greed appears to be one of the most prevalent nouns in many industries.

I can just imagine an honest but greedy leadership group developing their guiding principle—"Ensuring high profits and lavish salaries to every senior leader, at any cost to family life, health and integrity." Let us not forget when we're developing our guiding principle (s), that they should be the truth.

Although the primary goal of this book is to articulate the value of building teams using self-mastery, it's important that every employee knows and understands the mission of an organization. It's also important for every employee to fully comprehend the expectations set forth for their behavior and performance. Harmony in the workplace is as essential as productivity. People must know from the start that bad behavior and a lack of accountability will not be tolerated. People must also receive feedback and that feedback should be a common occurrence. Feedback is not provided solely by words but by non-verbal communication such as body language, facial expressions and posture. If an employee is waiting for their performance appraisal to receive feedback about their performance, their leader is falling short of his or her role. The performance appraisal should never be a surprise and it should always be a positive experience. Even when the appraisal reviews a 30-60-90-day work plan, or other verbal or written warnings, the experience should be positive. Just because an employee may not be suited for a particular position or organization does not mean they don't have a heart and are sensitive to their shortcomings and are good people. I am a proponent of the 360 degree evaluation. This type of evaluation not only includes knowledge and skill set, but it also includes the intangibles related to the core values that are exhibited on a daily basis. This type of evaluation is completed by many or all members of a work group or company. The people selected to complete 360 evaluations on their peers is dependent upon the position of the employee and the exposure of their skills and attitude within the organization. The jury is still out for me on whether 360 evaluations should be anonymous or not. Anonymity does allow for complete honesty without fear of any repercussions. It also opens a door for people to be inconsiderate and sometimes nasty, instead of providing constructive, productive feedback. When constructive advice is given, it can be very helpful to understand the perceptions of peers. A 360 evaluation builds a culture of accountability. They should be taken in the spirit they are intended. Leaders often make difficult decisions. The 360 is not a popularity assessment but it does assist a leader and employees to identify areas of excellence and those with the potential for growth.

Terminations can also be relatively positive. Just because it didn't work out, does not mean the employee's future is bleak. It should be presented as a learning experience with the situation occurring for the highest good of that individual. In most instances, the learning experience touched more lives than just the non-performing employee.

A good leader provides feedback on a continual basis. Feedback is feedback, positive or negative. Can you imagine a college basketball game with no score? The best player on the team may say, "It seems like I did well today." We are creatures that need feedback. Leaders must have the courage and commitment to provide feedback. They must take the time to be proactive and anticipate personnel and departmental needs. If a leader doesn't understand how to make a disciplinary action positive, they should seek assistance.

Mary Schechter and I recite our mission and guiding principles in all our "Leaders of Light" radio shows. Our tag line is "Self-Mastery: Becoming a Leader of Light in a Changing World." Our archived shows can be found on www.co-creatornetwork.com or can be searched for on iTunes by putting Mary or my name in the search box. There are many free podcasts. For those who may not be familiar, our guiding principles are: 1) We are ONE and life is a process of remembering who we are and why we are here; 2) We are only limited by the boundaries we place on ourselves; 3) Things are not always what they appear to be; and 4) There's a highest good for everything that happens in life and we must be grateful for everything.

Leaders are drawn to organizations that resonate with them. A leader will be attracted to organizations whose dominant behaviors harmonize with the beliefs and values they possess. As a leader traverses the road to self-mastery, the organizations that once felt appropriate may fall out of sync. Employees are drawn to organizations that resonate with them, too. The hiring process is different in a culture of self-mastery because the "emotional quotient" of candidates becomes as important as the "intelligence quotient." Within the new paradigm of leadership, the interview process includes an intuitive knowing of the emotional maturity and level of self-mastery that the candidate possesses. A positive attitude and a genuinely optimistic outlook on life will add light and luster to a work group. It's important to hire the correct skill set, but given two moderately equal candidates, the choice should always be the candidate with the higher emotional quotient. The emotional quotient can be likened to the level of self mastery that has been achieved or those characteristics that are not cerebral in nature and related to IQ but are emotional in nature and often reflect a person's self-actualization. Although there is controversy regarding the EQ, as there is no test to measure this value, ask any great leader and they'll tell you they know it when they see it. They make every effort to hire it and retain it, as those individuals are most successful and make significant contributions to the workplace.

Chapter Thirteen

The Family of Leaders and the Kitchen Table

Teams, like families are dysfunctional because of the characteristics they display when they are gathered together to make decisions and act as a unified system. In families, we know that people may be influenced by genetics, birth order, parental interaction and disciplinary styles, socioeconomic status, and exposure to tragedy, challenge, health issues, wellness, nutritional influences, etc. As we have discussed, the dynamics of a team are produced and dependent upon the characteristics of the people who comprise the group. Teams are made up of the same people who are among the family members described a few sentences ago. They have developed their cognitive/thinking style, problem solving skills, resiliency, and outlook on life from their initiation into their families, kindergarten class, grammar school, middle school, high school, college, etc. They present to the team as a reflection of their life's journey. There are a plethora of successful books on the market related to the dysfunctions and building of teams. It is helpful to study the dysfunctions of teams and work together in groups to overcome trust and communication barriers, while setting goals and objectives and defining team oriented strategic initiatives.

The maximum potential for overcoming team dysfunction will be within the self-discovery journey of the individuals that comprise that team. The underlying factors that influence trust and communication reside within the baggage of self. I repeat, the underlying factors that influence trust and communication reside within the baggage of self. The primary objective of this book is to illuminate the potentials within the self-mastery journey to not only improve daily life but build the best teams and inspire people to recognize the resources and tools within themselves. A leader and a person who occupies a leadership position are two different kinds of people. I'm sure the age old question of whether a leader is born or made has been the subject of many debates. In the 36 years I have been in the working world, and this includes my first summer job when I was 16 years old, I have met few leaders. I have met many well intentioned, bright and technically skilled people in leadership positions. I have met many nice people that have worked in an organization for many years who escalated to leadership positions because they did their time with true commitment and dedication. I have also met many people who like to manage other people and events and do so with good intentions. In all my years, however, I have known few true leaders. Leaders who could create, intuit, communicate, prepare, direct, manifest, motivate, perform, organize, serve and love. A true leader loves what they do, the organization they do it for and the people they serve. They are not exhausted by the daily challenges stimulated by the people and events around them. They have an innate ability to lead—a natural tendency to be successful among the potential of chaos. They usually have charismatic personalities and an abundance of integrity that many will seek to emulate. A person can absolutely work towards being a good leader. They can read, study, experience and integrate aspects of a good leader into who they want to become. They can train their thought processes to think and react in a fashion they wish to emulate from great leaders. An innate leader, however, will always be noticed, even if that innate leader is not in a leadership position. Not everyone who possesses the innate ability to lead desires a position of leadership.

This book is about building winning teams through self-mastery, but the concepts traverse every angle life offers. The concept that the team will be as viable and effective as the sum of its parts is simple. The journey, however, to overcome our insecurities and self-sabotaging cognitive styles is another story. It will be difficult if and when a person thinks it's going to be difficult. The person, who sincerely relinquishes their uncertainty to their higher power, will transcend with the greatest ease.

A leader may buy into this theory but they may not feel it is their place or the organization's place to interfere or be involved in the self-discovery journey of an employee. This is where the old paradigm of this type of thought process needs to be updated. A leader does not need to be involved in the psychoanalysis of an employee or become a part of their healing journey and travel within the roads of privacy. They should, however, support the concept and bring opportunities into the work environment for this self-discovery to be facilitated and/or supported. I can see a specialty in social work developing in the future. At our practice, we have a tremendous benefit in having social workers employed. These social workers are there for the patients, but I can't tell you how many times they have brought clarity of thought and emotion to our employees (this includes me). It's great to have Employee Assistance Programs (EAPs) that offer counseling, but often the employees get wrapped up in their work and personal and family responsibilities and don't have the time or fortitude to follow-up with the EAPs. Doctors will tell you, when it's all under one roof, you get better patient compliance. Owners of grocery stores that include pharmacies, bakeries, book nooks, home furnishings, natural and organic foods, beer and wine and other non-grocery options will agree with the impact of the "everything under one roof" concept, too.

When it comes to teams, however, team building that occurs on both an individual and group basis is imperative to maximize effectiveness. Replacing leaders can be even more expensive than replacing workers, so a commitment to hire the right individuals and keep them fulfilled is paramount. Individual leadership and life coaching should commence at the top with the executive leadership team and it should be introduced by and include the owner/CEO/boss. A consultant or facilitator with incredible insight, intuition, wisdom and experience in personal self-help and organizational development works best. If this person also possesses a sharp business acumen, it's even better.

During a leadership meeting or any meeting, it's not uncommon for one person to make a comment or bring up a subject that is not taken within the spirit it was intended. The comment may be interpreted as offensive and upset one or more colleagues. When group emotions dominate, the effectiveness of the whole begins to be compromised. Subsequent to the meeting, the comment is given life as it births into the subject of future communications between and among members of the leadership team. Time and energy is wasted, productivity is diminished, harmony is compromised and segregation commences. The leadership team officially has energy forces pulling members in different directions. Once in awhile, there will be one person who is clueless about this occurrence—namely the person who made the comment or brought up the subject. They can be clueless for a few reasons. Perhaps nobody has had the courage to speak to them about the comment and resulting negative ramifications. Another possibility is because their intention was never to be divisive, disrespectful or hurtful, the spray of negativity caused by their comment falls outside their scope of awareness. Perhaps they lack the intuitive skills to notice what really happened at the meeting and anticipate the separation of team members and the waste of energy that was instigated. Just to be clear, if it was the leader's intention to hurt another leader or diminish the value of the team, that's another story. If that's the case, the person in charge of that leader needs to make some serious assessments as to whether that individual is right for the team.

Going back to our meeting scenario, the best of situations would have been for the individual who was confused or hurt by the comment to speak up immediately or speak to the individual after the meeting—perhaps after some time to cool off or just contemplate the situation. We often find it easier to express our feelings to somebody else who was at the meeting, but if it's not the person who instigated the upset, the result can be more divisive than fruitful, and that is almost always not the intention of anyone. To speak up in a meeting, there must be an environment of trust, a feeling of support and a level of comfort that speaking one's truth is accepted. There must also be an environment where people agree to disagree and where the good of the whole supersedes the good of any one individual. There can't be hidden and/or personal agendas. The agenda always needs to be "united we're successful and divided isn't an option." Success is only achieved when it's measured by the cumulative success of the group—as soon as one person is not successful, the group is not successful. The dynamic has to be such that no matter what happens behind closed doors at meetings, when the leadership team walks out the door, everyone is on the same page, singing the same song, supporting and encouraging each leader's success. Since intentions of people are easily misunderstood, it's also imperative that a depth of trust among leadership team members fosters an environment where potential or brewing misunderstandings outside the leadership group are nipped in the bud because each leader acts as a back-up for clarity. In other words, the truth and purity of the good intentions of people are protected within the work environment. Each leader must have each other's best interest at heart and must be ready at a moment's notice to defend their colleague when the potential for misunderstandings develop. For example, it's important for me to know what is in the mind and hearts of those leaders that report to me. I am intuitive and can usually recognize the potential for other employees to misinterpret the intentions of the leaders. Perhaps the leader's choice of words or the actions they displayed when conveying a piece of information or during a particular situation were less than optimal for a cohesive response. Everyone is human and we all have days when our judgment may fall a notch. I try to be quick to add clarity to the situation by restating intention. My confidence in knowing the leader's intention comes from knowing who they are and trusting them.

When people have shared many aspects of themselves with each other, they develop a higher level of comfort that allows their intentions to be better understood and trusted. It's similar to knowing someone so well you can read their mind or predict how they will respond to any given situation. It takes time, energy and commitment between and among every team member to share enough of themselves with each other to understand the basis of where and how thoughts originate.

To develop an environment where the team is unified, the members of the group need to understand their individual personal cognitive style. They need an acute awareness of their level of rationality and/or irrationality within their self-talk and their patterns of thought and emotions. They need to know the sources of how their perceptions are created and the background and quality of the lens in which they view life. Self-evaluation becomes essential. An individual needs to understand their fears and insecurities. They need to figure out to whom they give the power to create their emotions and feelings and why. They also need to develop a level of basic understanding and respect for other people's cognitive styles and basis for actions. All these suggestions require a trip within the recesses of the self and a level of communication with others to understand and respect their perspectives. This can occur with a desire to traverse the self-mastery journey and spend enough time with the work group to share parts of themselves. This type of sharing makes people feel vulnerable so the commitment to want to share must strongly exist. The purpose and desired outcome to go the length of the field, outside of one's comfort zones must be known and worth the risk of being vulnerable. The correct mix of people on the team is essential. For the leadership team to reach these heights of performance, everyone on the team should fit together like a complete puzzle. Regardless of how solid a team becomes, however, with complacency, there is always the potential for misunderstandings to occur and issues to fester. The commitment to continue to grow individually and together never ends and like all partnerships, it always requires work.

One of my 8½ x 11s from years past was the word "Link." I had an old, worn out paper bag with me. The first item I removed from the bag was a shiny, metal linked chain. I held up the chain and said, "This chain, with its shiny metal links can be used to lift heavy objects. It is impervious to most caustic agents and it's strong and durable. It is capable of handling many tough jobs." The second item I removed from the bag was a yellow, hard plastic linked chain. I held up the second chain and said, "This chain, with its hard, durable, yellow plastic links can be used to lift moderately heavy objects. It is not as impervious as the shiny metal chain, but it's still strong. It is capable of handling some tough jobs." The third item I removed from the old paper bag was a pretty paper chain made from various colors of construction paper. I held up the chain and said, "This chain, with its pretty colors is made of paper. It's rather fragile and really can't lift too many items. It's delicate and its durability can't compare to the two other chains. It is not appropriate for any type of tough job but it can hang around and look nice." I continued talking about how during life—and even sometimes during the same day—we become those links on the chain. Sometimes we're tough and impervious, sometimes we're moderately prepared for the job and sometimes, we're fragile. The strength and power of the team is only as strong as the weakest link. I used an old idiom to make this analogy but the illustration was powerful. The only way to become those shiny, metal links is to build up mass and imperviousness through the journey inside the self. If we are strong and resilient on the inside, it will be reflected on the outside and our partnerships, friendships, families, workgroups and communities will be stronger and more resourceful with the capability to handle the tough jobs.

Although most of us had been together for years, 2010 was a year of transformation for our senior leadership group. Mentally, emotionally and spiritually, we traveled where few teams have ventured and the rewards have been many. Like the self-mastery journey, this evolution of the team is never ending. Although we were a highly functioning team, really got along well and genuinely liked each other, we had not reached the level of effectiveness, mastery and oneness in our teamwork that we knew was attainable. Today, I can honestly say we are not perfect but we maintain a level of understanding about ourselves and each other that few teams reach. What distinguishes us from others is awareness, commitment and courage. In early 2010, in addition to our focus on operations, our team also focused on the emotional parameters that run beneath the surface and code our individual and team oriented behavior and actions. At this point in our national and international development, it may be rare to find a leadership team that maintains a commitment to this perspective, but the future will necessitate a different paradigm. I believe we exemplify that style today. We understand and trust each other at levels that have surpassed our original intentions. It did not come without effort, risk and some discomfort. A fundamental characteristic of this risk was that it was doused with vulnerability. People had to share things about themselves and reveal aspects of their personality and thinking style that are usually hidden from conversation but silently catalyze actions. As we truly develop trust and faith in a colleague's intention, we begin to understand that the sparks that ignite anger and adversity are self inflicted from the embers of our past that burn within our own psyche. We begin to develop an awareness of how we breathe the fire of life into the smoldering ashes of adversity because of the reflection of ourselves that other people provide. The shadow created by our ego is like dust upon our mirror of self discovery. When a colleague is trusted as a genuine advocate and team player, the intention to hurt is always a misunderstanding that is not real. It is imperative to build the team with the right people. Their core must be trustworthy and honest and the desire to hurt must not exist. When the right people are on the team, they will not intentionally sabotage other people or the team. There are leaders in this world who prefer and foster the dog-eat-dog style of leadership. They are convinced it is good for profit margins. I'll tell you that I think it's least desirable for the evolution of spirit—which is the most important goal of our existence. In the end, the evolution of spirit will be that which we care most about.

In 2009, I felt the need to trim down the number of leaders that attended our regularly scheduled senior leadership meetings. We had achieved many successes together, but it was evident that to reach the next level, the group needed to be smaller. The group needed to be smaller in number for a few reasons that included but were not limited to: the potential for especially difficult and painful decisions was lurking in the future and a smaller number of people had more potential to work together effectively; it's difficult for too many people to agree on something; and I knew we were headed for team building exercises that would rip the masks of fear from our being and it's difficult to be vulnerable in a larger group. The new leadership group needed to comprise a cross section of every department, however, and a full caste of expertise needed to be present. Our new leadership team was ultimately created to include all Chief positions and two director level leaders. After some thought, the new name I gave to this panel of leaders was the "Kitchen Table" or "KT" gang. Including myself, there are eight (8) members in total—eight people who have revealed elements of their life and thought processes that most leadership groups would shun away from revealing. I am grateful to my leadership team. The commitment and courage that we all demonstrate is not always easy but it's worth the effort. We will always have speed bumps in the road on our mastery journey as individuals and as a team. The effort put forth needs to be constant because when a team thinks they've arrived and stop paying attention, dysfunction has an opportunity to slide in. Somehow, we went out on a limb—perhaps as an experiment to ourselves. We are stronger and more united and when you progress far enough on the team journey, there's no going back.

When I grew up, all the important decision occurred at the kitchen table. Kitchen tables are very important to Italians and I presume they're equally important to most other families. It's the safe place where agreements and disagreements are allowed to occur among family members. It's the safe place where laughter and tears may be shared. It's the place where honesty and admirable values underscore the objectives of discourse. It's where the family gathers. It's where tough conversations and decisions are made. A family is the group that trusts one another and walks out of the kitchen loving and protecting each other, even if the dialog that just transpired was heated and uncomfortable—even when the family is not biologically related. The kitchen table is where you say what's on your mind and you share that part of yourself that only the "family" is honored to witness. The kitchen table is where you plan your strategies and figure out who is going to do what and how it's going to get done most effectively and lovingly. How blessed am I to not just have a senior leadership team but to have a "KT" or "Kitchen Table" gang. When the KT first gathered, I explained the commitment that went with the title. We started out with a name, now we are a family—a family of leaders united in our spirit, our mission, our guiding principles and our values. A family of leaders that work for the good of the whole and who make the world a better place, one person at a time, from the inside-out.

Chapter Fourteen

The Tool box within the self

Every tool for self-mastery can be found within the self. The tools to become a great leader can be found in the same place. It's common to seek resources and references when embarking on a new project or chapter in life. When I found out I was pregnant, for example, I went shopping and purchased a number of books on pregnancy—what to expect, how the fetus was developing, how to prepare physically and emotionally, etc. I am an avid reader and I love to gather perspectives of other people. I believe that gathering data to make informed decisions is essential. Knowledge and wisdom imparted from others is an integral part of life, but it is paramount to gather information, file it, but make your own decisions. Since the path of life is unique and the circumstances that surround each facet of life can never be known by another, we are our best advocates and advisors. This is what makes each of our paths unique and acceptable. One journey will never be the same as another so the answers we seek and the path we travel needs to be our own. Our comparison to others has the potential to precipitate judgment, inferiority and frustration or a feeling that we're better than somebody else. If we believe that there is highest good for everything that happens to us, then every path is just as it should be, given the time and circumstances. It's great to seek knowledge and data elsewhere, but the wisdom of the self should never be superseded. For that reason, it's essential to have confidence that we were born with tools, innate skills and abilities to assist ourselves on the paths we have chosen to take. I don't think we forgot to pack before we left to arrive on planet earth. I think we packed everything we needed and nothing that comes our way is too much for us to handle, even if some days we wonder how we're going to make it another day.

The self-mastery journey would be the destination if there was a destination. This never-ending journey from the inside-out, however, continues through lifetimes. If you are a person who believes that we have lived other lifetimes on earth, perhaps you will ponder the following. If we think outside the box of being human, and we open our minds to fathom the knowledge and wisdom that may be accessible to us if we were to tap into the experiences of all our lifetimes, one could acquire a glimpse of the potential that may exist to access a vast array of knowledge, wisdom and experience. This knowledge, wisdom and experience would prove to be invaluable, especially in the work place. This ability would initially depend upon the openness of the mind and belief that such potential can exist. Once again, I'll remind you, we are only limited by the boundaries we place on ourselves. We often let others influence the boundaries we place on ourselves, especially being limited by the parameters set forth by people and religions we love and hold dear to our heart. Have you ever contemplated how many beliefs you hold true because somebody else told you they were true? Have you ever contemplated the magnitude of the transfer of information into your thoughts and your life from those you loved and loved you that resulted from generations of hand-me-down beliefs? As soon as we can talk and understand, those that love us and care for us, teach us what they believe is true and correct. They teach us the words and symbols of life and they assist in molding us into the adults they hope we will become. In some instances, the innocence and love that resides in the developing child is snuffed away from those experiences. Some people grow old without ever contemplating who they really are. They just accept what others have told and shown them through the years, and they demonstrate behavior yielded from those influences. Some people let others define who they are instead of exploring that complexity themselves. Some feel a void but don't seek to understand why the void exists. Sometimes, instead of filling the void with what we need, we fill it with what feels good. From the time we are children, others are generous to let us know what they think of us. The brutality of grammar and middle school can be challenging to forget. The inadequacies of the teen years often create wounds that are difficult to heal. The torments of relationships are often allowed to lay groundwork for future beliefs regarding the self. When all challenges are viewed as opportunities for growth, immersed in situations and with people that we have chosen on some level of soul, we can see the blessings and good fortunes that rest within the density of life and we will be inspired to feel and live a life of immense gratitude.

Resiliency is a key factor to overcoming obstacles when life just doesn't proceed as planned, expected or desired. Resiliency is linked to a person's style of thinking, their language of internal thought, and the approach they use with problem solving. It is related to a person's ability to break down huge chunks of challenge into smaller, more manageable pieces. Resiliency is connected to a person's outlook on life and the value they place on themselves and the purpose of obstacles. When a person believes there is a reason for everything and that reason always follows the path to nurture one's self-development, challenges become opportunities, regardless of the depths of adversity one may experience. When a person believes challenges provide opportunities to develop and maintain fortitude within the self to always move forward, through difficult times, overcoming obstacles and finding the blessing in every moment of despair, they develop the resiliency to play whatever hand of cards life has dealt them in a positive and formative manner. If we contemplate this spiritually, accepting the concept of the co-created plan and understanding that the soul must agree and accept these challenges before they can occur, one can find the silver lining in every cloud and resiliency can be deepened.

We all have opinions on how the world should work and how people should act, react and conform to societal norms. There are those who are carefree and easy going and then there are those coiled quite tightly. Some people are open minded and flexible in the acceptance of people and events while others are closed minded and judgmental. We often judge others the way we consciously or unconsciously judge ourselves. Expectations are often placed on ourselves, people and life in general and when these expectations are not met, anger and disappointment follow. Deeply held beliefs within the recesses of the unconscious mind may surface to instigate feelings and emotions that we don't fully understand and our level of resiliency may suffer as a result of this. These unconscious beliefs may have been instilled during childhood or difficult situations in life and may cause a person to overreact to the little things in life that should not rock their boat and provoke the high levels of anxiety that occur. It's helpful to evaluate how we under-react, react and over-react to situations that occur in life. When a person delves deeper into situations in which they under-react and are rather numb or over-react and exhibit overdrive responses, it can help to illuminate patterns that need healing.

We have the tools within ourselves to increase our resiliency. When confronted with a challenge, it's helpful to listen to our thoughts and identify the types of words, phrases and general internal dialog that are commonplace during these situations. When a person pays attention to how these thoughts make them feel, they can begin to understand the cascade of physical, mental and emotional effects that occur during this communication with the self. It may be helpful to write down these thoughts and analyze them. What kinds of words are they? Are they negative or positive? Do they foster hope or despair? Are they words of blame and if so, who is blamed when things don't go the way a person desires? Who or what rests between you and your success? To whom or to what are you giving power to prevent you from obtaining your desired outcome? What kind of conclusions about the self and life are identified? Are assumptions commonplace during this dialog? Is the style of thought working well or sabotaging happiness and inner peace?

It's essential to stay calm and focused when feeling overwhelmed in any situation. When anything is too complex, be it a challenge at the office or at home, when the challenge is broken down into understandable and manageable parts, resolution is facilitated. We can train ourselves to stay calm and focused. A sense of calm can be felt amidst the chaos when we organize our thoughts and surroundings. It's also essential to remember to b-r-e-a-t-h-e. A person can reach out for help from friends or loved ones. One can seek professional counseling that will assist in the analysis of internal dialog and the habits of thought that disrupt relationships and cause anxiety. Our level of success and happiness in life is related to our resiliency and how we cope with change, stress and challenge. We can increase our resiliency by training ourselves to identify our thought patterns and understand how we view and attempt to solve problems. We can improve our prioritization skills and develop coping mechanisms. The self-mastery journey increases resiliency by the nature of its personal and spiritual growth.

Becoming the observer is another important tool. I have often thought how well I am able to give advice to others but how poorly I sometimes give it to myself. When I shared that concept with others, I found that just about everyone agreed that their experience was the same. It appears to be much easier to give advice to another person than to ourselves. When I have contemplated the reason for this, the number one reason that comes to mind is that when we give advice to others, we are always the observer. This observer is not consumed or likely affected by the past and the plethora of details an issue may be swimming in. The observer is not worried or engrossed in the past or future. It is impossible for the observer to possess the emotions or feelings driving a situation, because they don't have that level of history and detail. An observer is focused on the issue at hand and is evaluating in the present tense—the now. The observer is firmly planted in the present moment, commonly evaluating the situation in a more global and objective manner. The helpful nature of the observer is a direct result of the aforementioned characteristics. Since the observer role works so well, it can be an essential tool for self-mastery, and for building resiliency. To become the observer for oneself, a person needs to find their own way to facilitate this separation so they can effectively "step out of the self."

There are ways to step outside oneself to become the observer, but it may require creativity. No matter how it's done, a person needs to step outside themselves and commit to observing and not enabling the self. This can be done in a variety of creative ways and the imagination is very helpful when performing in this role. For example, a person can journal what is going on and articulate every aspect of the challenge from the thoughts to the emotions that are running rampant. Subsequently, that person can step aside, perhaps wait some time, and go back and read the journal and comment as though it belonged to somebody else.

A person can set the table with two cups of tea or two glasses of wine. It's always fun (although it sounds weird) to talk to an invisible person (or you could invite one of your favorite spirits or light beings to join you) to get out all the "stuff" that's bothering you. It's inexpensive and sometimes just releasing that which is pent up inside alleviates stress and anxiety. Another option is handing the journal over to the other side of the table. When the person hands over the journal to the other side of the table, they can physically get up, move into the other chair, pretend to be somebody else and review the journal with objectivity. The observer may need to exemplify tough love, trying not to enable. Enabling doesn't help anyone move out of the checker square.

When we become the observer, we can remove ourselves from the emotion and be that honest friend that offers us sound advice with one added value. In this instance, the observer knows us to our core and we can't hide, embellish or make up stories to fool the observer. It's not always easy being honest with ourselves but if we love ourselves the way we should, we will be the best friend we can have in problem solving.

Communication is essential and we possess the tools to break any communication barrier between and among ourselves and other people. Since we can only control ourselves we can't force anybody to communicate with us but we can change our expectations by changing the way we think. Quality is an aspect that is often neglected within the choice of words. America runs at top speed and text messaging and emails fly voluminously throughout the day. Without voice and the inflection of words, a dimension of quality communication is diminished and the potential for miscommunication is high. A moment more of thought can reduce the potential for misdirected intentions.

The spoken word has incredible potential to slice and dice. We should all make every effort to select our words wisely and our intention should always be to put quality in our communication. Tone of voice and the inflection in our rhythm of speech are integral components of the quality of our communication. Nonverbal communication is void in many of our modes of communication and attention to the quality of words becomes more important when that dimension is nonexistent. Non-verbal communication often conveys as much information as words. Facial expressions and body language lends significant meaning to communication.

Great leaders are master communicators. They are expert readers of facial expressions, body language, verbal tones and voice inflections. They understand human nature and can anticipate how certain types of communication will be received by others. They understand the importance of communication, especially proactive communication. A leader is keenly aware of what kind of circumstances or dialog will inflame, insult, and instigate insecurity. They are committed to proactive communication and early dialog to prevent misunderstandings. They know that the time needed to proactively communicate, even if it sometimes proves to be exhausting, is less than the time and effort required to extinguish issues when they're in full burn due to a lack of communication or the development of misperceptions. Breaking down barriers of communication is a strong point of a great leader. They recognize that communication is one of the most fundamental and significant keys to every successful relationship, workgroup and organization. A great leader can appear to see into the future, as their experience, wisdom and intuition allows them to predict and proactively prevent personnel and operational issues before they start. They will intuitively see areas that have the potential to incite conflict and they will prevent these conflicts from occurring by communicating effectively with all people involved. This is one of the natural gifts of an innate leader and one of the characteristics that budding leaders need to acknowledge and enhance in their leadership style.

Clearing clutter is another great tool to assist the self in the mastery journey. Physical clutter has a way of confusing and scattering one's mind. I know many people love a cluttered office as they feel comfortable with the surrounding valuable debris, but organizing one's surroundings and clearing clutter can adjust an attitude away from chaos and anxiety. Clearing the clutter within and allowing yourself to be an open channel of love to yourself and others is an integral part of the mastery journey.

Mindfulness is the art of paying attention and maintaining a deep awareness of everything that is happening in the present moment. This awareness in endogenous and exogenous, meaning that this acute level of awareness takes place on the inside and outside. Everyone is capable of being and becoming more mindful. Like any exercise, it gets easier the more you do it. Mindfulness in the state of gratitude creates a level of inner peace and harmony.

To be mindful of our words allows us to focus on the quality we place in our communication. To be mindful of what we're eating, allows us to see beyond what the food is and become the food. I love oranges and one of my favorite mindful eating exercises is eating an orange, slowly and by myself with no place to run. It is a great experience for me to take my time and savor the delicious, sweet taste and texture of the orange. It's so beautiful in color and vibrant in smell and I love to focus on the precious arrangement of pulp, filled with life that is a gift and treat for us to enjoy. An orange is so friendly. I love to break a slice in half and stare at the arrangement of the shapes and curves, and pay attention how it feels inside to slow down and eat this friendly snack. You may think I'm making way too big a deal out of this orange. But it's a way to pay attention to the now and slow down and practice mindfulness. Even if you only do this once a year, the process rests in a greater state of awareness.

Like many others, I try to be more mindful of life—to smell the roses instead of just running by them, weeding around them or trimming them while getting angry as the thorns try to poke through my rubber gardening gloves. Have you ever really stared at a rose petal—soaked in its beauty and the gift it provides to our life, along with the millions of other miracles around us? Being mindful is a great way to reduce stress and fall in love with the gifts of this Universe. Enriching our mindfulness enriches our knowing of oneness and the interconnectedness of all people and things.

Intuition is another essential tool of which birth has gifted us. When a person or leader accesses their intuition, they have an advantage over those who do not recognize or utilize this tool. Intuition provides a sixth sense, equally important as sight, smell, sound, taste and touch. Intuition and spirituality are intertwined and interconnected. As one grows more spiritual, a more enriched intuition develops as a byproduct. As one focuses on enriching their intuitive skills, enriched spirituality follows. I like to think of intuition as the language of spirit in a 3D world. In business, as with all situations, intuition is one of the most important tools we can utilize as leaders. As we utilize and exercise this gift, it becomes stronger and more profound. Meditation and contemplation are great tools to enhance intuition. Pausing and paying attention to the messages we receive while acknowledging confirmation of our intuitive knowing allows us to gain trust in our ability to connect to our higher selves and the forces of light; the light of love that envelops our world.

Chapter Fifteen

The Mind's Balance Sheet

In the journey of self mastery and development as a great leader, a heightened awareness of the presence of the ego or higher self and the role they play in life is essential. It is important to possess a conscious awareness and understanding of which of these elements of the self is in control at any given moment in time. It's especially important to understand which one gets more playing time on the field of life. Patterns of thinking are habit forming and it behooves a person to recognize whether the path of ego or higher self is more habitual. An easy way I can tell which direction my thoughts are being created is by how it feels inside. When I am in chaos or I'm miserable or irritable or angry or confused, if I take a moment to do a self evaluation of what server is driving my thoughts, it's usually clear to me that my ego is in overdrive. When I'm filled with love and my heart is jumping for joy, I know I'm connecting with my higher self.

When people maintain a positive attitude, especially in the face of adversity, it's likely the work of the higher self. There are no victims when the higher self is in control. I have known religious people who hide behind their dogmatic beliefs of goodness to justify judgmental and sometimes mean behavior. I have also known extremely religious, miserable people. It could be just me, but I am yet to meet a spiritually evolved, miserable person. An occasional bad mood is not what I'm referring to—I'm referring to miserable people who exude negative energy and drain the energy of others when in close proximity. Sometimes I think dogmatic rules and regulations have left people inflexible to human frailty and have made them think they're exempt from being accountable for every thought. I have heard many voices of god that can only be derived from a human tongue.

The habit of positive thinking is related to a constant connection to the wise and divine aspect of ourselves. An essential choice we make every iota of every second of every minute of the day is allowing or ego or higher self to reign supreme. As spiritual beings having a physical experience, the first choice in our co-created plan was to birth on planet earth, the "Free-Will Planet." The earth is our playground to create thoughts and make our own choices. Our earthly reminder of our connection to spirit resides in our intuition. We should rely on our intuition as readily as our eyes, ears and spreadsheets.

In business, the balance sheet is an important piece of information that is routinely evaluated. A balance sheet is one of the financial indicators, representing a given moment in time that demonstrates and organizes the assets, liabilities and net worth or equity of a legal entity. It provides an important piece of information that must be assessed on a continual basis to ensure solvency, longevity and fortitude.

Many years ago, as I began to understand the ego and the higher self and roles they play in my life, I developed, what I term, *The Mind's Balance Sheet* and I've found it very helpful. At that time, I was trying to gain a better understanding of whether my ego or higher self was sitting in the control center. Up until that point, I never gave much thought to which part of me was engaged or placed on autopilot and I'm not sure I even knew the differences. The only similarity my Mind's Balance Sheet has to a financial balance sheet is that is represents one moment in time and compares two indices. In the business format, it's assets and liabilities, in mine, it's ego and higher self.

As was discussed in Chapter Three, the ego is that part of us that is earthly in nature. When any situation occurs, the lens in which we perceive and interpret events is biased by our ego. The self-talk that is produced when we interpret the stimuli of life, is a product of our egos and/or higher selves. To understand which algorithm has been activated, it's necessary to identify and examine the emotions and feelings that occur in the body. To me, the higher self is the God self. It is the wise and trusted mentor that is constantly loving and protecting. It is the part of us that will always take the high road. It is the part of us that will always seek our higher good, in conjunction with the highest good of the whole. The higher self is the producer of loving thoughts, happiness and internal peace. The ego is the whirling dervish that makes us think that things are happening to us instead of just happening. The ego is that part of us that will elicit self-talk that tells us we're not good enough, liked enough, or worthy enough. The higher self is the part of us that will always be tolerant and loving. The ego is the part that is connected to fear. The higher self is the part connected and dedicated to love.

We can choose to give power to our higher selves. We can practice relinquishing our authority to choose and direct our higher self to control our decisions. We can do this at home, at work and anyplace in between. We can do it with all aspects of life or only certain ones. We can do it with food. We can combine our knowledge of good nutrition and healthy habits and give our eating decision making capabilities to our higher self. We can ask that we are intuitively directed to eat only those foods that are in the best interest of our good health and wellness. We can always elect not to listen to our higher self, but it's easier than one would think to give power to that divine part of ourselves. Like many things, it's about practice. The more we practice understanding which burner is fired, the ego or higher self, the easier we will recognize what's going on inside ourselves. We can have our higher self enter any relationship and ask for guidance in circumstances of passion or conflict. When our higher selves drive the bus we intuitively know that we are heading in a direction that is good for us. We can feel the alignment with our highest good and it manifests as peace and joy, even amidst difficult challenges. When practicing to become the observer, it's especially helpful to be the observer while tapping into our higher self and allowing those thoughts to flow into our consciousness.

The following illustration is a pictorial depiction of my *Minds Balance Sheet*. We are able to hit the "pause" button anytime we wish to evaluate our status. When we are thinking with our higher self, our God-self, our spiritual self, the happy face connotes the level of happiness and inner peace we may be feeling. The large "1" connotes a feeling of oneness is strong and we are connected to life in the most vibrant of ways. When the ego reigns supreme, the sad face connotes a

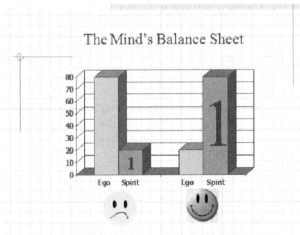

The Mind's Balance Sheet

level of frustration and anxiety or stress and the small "1" indicates our distance from the knowing and feeling of oneness. When this exercise is routinely practiced such that the pause button is hit during various times of the day, it builds awareness of our thought patterns and subsequent emotions and feelings. After time, it becomes a natural awareness such that when the ego is driving the bus, the substitution to the higher self is automatic, without cognitive thought and effort.

Chapter Sixteen

Consciousness

The self mastery journey is accelerated if a person has an understanding of the roles and levels of consciousness. It's helpful for a leader to understand the same, as it makes a difference in individual and group dynamics. Throughout the day, we respond to the magnitude and variety of stimuli that life dishes out to us. Moment to moment we respond, respond and respond. How we respond effects our mood, the tone and tenor of our life, and our future. Many proceed through life not consciously aware of the backbone of aggregate data that writes code and runs in the background. This code directs our perceptions and flavors our responses and is known as the subconscious mind. Many fail to recognize that they have the power to consciously create the life before them instead of just responding, responding and responding. Understanding the levels of consciousness is an integral part of self-mastery. As we explore and discover issues that lie dormant in the unconscious recesses of our mind, we gain a conscious awareness of how we respond to stimuli around us. When we gain this awareness, we can heal wounds of the past, acknowledge the potential of tomorrow and create the existence we wish to have. This self-discovery leads to self-mastery as we understand how to gain self-control in our lives and go forth leading a positive and productive life.

Certified in Heart Centered Hypnotherapy through the Wellness Institute (Issaquah, WA), I have been privileged to journey into the superconscious, conscious and subconscious minds with my clients. I have witnessed dramatic improvement in how people interpret and respond to the stimuli of life—from developing an enriched self-esteem to improved relationships. I have been exposed to people healing their addictions. I have witnessed my clients recall tragic events in their life that were not accessible in their sphere of awareness because of the wall of protection they built to shelter themselves from the pain and suffering.

I have been present when the higher self and the conscious wise adult of an individual assisted in the healing of the inner child from physical, mental, and emotional neglect, abuse and/or abandonment. The levels of healing I have witnessed are not temporary; they are life altering and permanent. By taking a leap of faith and journeying into hypnotherapy, these precious adults healed the child within that had been silenced and wounded for many years. It is remarkable to witness a client on their journey into their subconscious mind as they learn of events and experiences that were totally and completely unknown to their conscious mind or conscious awareness. It also amazes me how often these wounds occurred in other lifetimes. The clarity of these journeys to other lifetimes is astounding to me and I'm so grateful for the trust my clients place in our relationship and the value of hypnotherapy. If I ever had a doubt that other lifetimes existed and could play a role in our current life, they were extinguished when I became a hypnotherapist. My spirituality has also been affected by what I have learned from hypnotherapy sessions. The importances we place on things in our life are sometimes just so unimportant.

Subsequent to these treatments, people are often amazed at what they discovered about themselves. They are also amazed to find out aspects of their infancy or childhood and adolescence years. They often learn things about their families and the people who were in positions to influence their early formative years. I have witnessed people developing great love and forgiveness for themselves and others after they became aware of deeply seeded issues that robbed them of their innocence and ability to grow into healthy, happy and well-balanced adults.

The conscious mind is the mind of awareness. It is the mind people think with—it is the realm of your mind you are using as you read this book. It's responsible for short term memory and processes a limited quantity of information as compared to the subconscious mind. The conscious mind makes the grocery list and plans dinner. Freud said that the conscious mind includes everything that is inside our awareness. He felt it's the part of our mind's processing whereby we could think and talk in a rational manner. The conscious mind includes memories, sensations, perceptions and fantasies that are within our awareness. It also includes information that is readily available that we may not be thinking of right now but we can access instantaneously. The conscious mind is logical and it prefers when things make sense and have a reason. It enjoys thinking linearly and in terms of cause and effect. The conscious mind is the author of self-talk but responds to the perceptions developed by the subconscious mind that are influenced by the data warehouse of stored experiences located there.

The subconscious mind houses long-term memory. It is the data warehouse of information that represents everything we have seen, heard, smelled, tasted, and felt. It is the part of our mind that holds emotions and feelings. It is the part that houses habits, patterns of thought and relationships. It is also the part of our mind where addictions are embedded and stored. It's the part of our mind that controls involuntary bodily functions such as our cardiac, respiratory and craniosacral rhythms. It is the creative part of us that influences our conscious mind. It is responsible for our developmental stages and our spiritual connections. The subconscious mind is capable of processing a magnitude of information simultaneously. It is the master multi-tasker within the recesses of our mind. It can make associations between and among bits of data instantaneously. The subconscious mind is unlimited in time and space and can access information from other lifetimes. I cannot express the times I have witnessed people obtain the answers to questions that resided in the conscious mind from their subconscious mind. The subconscious mind is literal and unlike the conscious mind that can analyze a given situation and decide if it's politically correct or in your best interest, the subconscious mind has no volition. It gathers data, stores it and processes it for fuel for the conscious mind. The subconscious mind does not know when something is good for us or bad for us; it just notes patterns and burns the grooves more deeply into the cascade of chemical reactions that serve the mind and body. We can be addicted to thoughts, behaviors, feelings or substances. A person can sabotage their best efforts for self growth and development. Subconscious beliefs may be running in the background of which we have no conscious awareness. We may know how we react to something or somebody, and we may know how often that occurs, but we may not know why.

The Wellness Institute teaches that the process of shifting back and forth between the conscious and subconscious mind is a natural process that occurs 80% of every day. Levels of consciousness span from fully alert to asleep. When a person begins to learn how to be still and relaxes the mind in meditation, they can deeply alter their state of consciousness. Even if we are not meditating or purposefully trying to alter our states of consciousness, we do it throughout the day. One of the simplest examples of altering our state of consciousness without trying can occur while we are driving our vehicles. I'm thankful for my navigation system for so many reasons, not the least of which allows me to see the name of the highway or street that I'm on at any given time—especially when I can't recall how or when I got there (not because I was drinking, but because I was thinking). Perhaps you are similar in that once and awhile you seem to wake up (come back to a fully alert state of consciousness) while you're driving, wondering exactly where you are, not recalling getting off of one highway and onto another? It is not uncommon to enter into a driver's hypnotic state whereby the subconscious mind takes over and transfers to autopilot to monitor everything and ensure safety. Learning how to drive is another great example, especially if a person is learning to drive a standard shift vehicle. In the beginning, a person may feel as though they can't pay enough attention, looking all around, trying to be aware of the environment, vehicles and traffic patterns, all while listening to the engine and transmission to know when to shift into a different gear. When experience is gained, the process and level of awareness as when to shift and how to drive becomes automatic. The subconscious mind is a great gift and maintains an endless supply of storage space.

The power of the superconscious mind has been written about for many years. The great Austrian psychoanalyst, Carl Jung felt that all the knowledge and wisdom of the ages was available to everyone through the superconscious mind. My explanation of the superconscious mind is best articulated through one of my personal experiences during my individual heart centered hypnotherapy session. As I entered the hypnotic trance, the question of a spiritual connection was asked of me. To my left was a being of light that I could only explain as huge. It appeared as an egg shaped light of about 12 feet tall. I had an instantaneous knowing of who and what this light represented and it was confirmed through communication with me. I was told that this light being represented the essence of my higher self. I knew it was that divine aspect of myself that was accessible at all times. I knew it was actually a form or essence of myself—yet the love that penetrated my heart from this being was so overwhelmingly profound and incredible that tears were exploding from my eyes and streaming down my face at rapid fire. I think it's difficult for the human mind to understand the essence of our being and the multifaceted nature of our existence. That's why I feel it's so important to maintain an open mind and be open to new revelations. When these revelations come from the inside-out, it can be extremely profound. This essence was a feminine energy and this energy explained that its age was around 4,000 years old. This presence remained silent though the 90 minute session, standing at my left side, as communication only occurred during the commencement of the hypnotherapy session. Although there was no further communication during the session, I could feel the love and protection throughout. In the session, to my right was my four year old inner child that needed to share some information and emotions with me. I could see this little girl so plainly and I felt like I was not only gaining an understanding of myself but of the relationship among my higher self or superconscious mind, my conscious mind and my subconscious mind. It was all so clear to me. All three were present and available and were segregated in a very unique and loving way. This experience was life altering for a variety of reasons, all of which I will remain eternally grateful. It occurred during the intensive hypnotherapy certification training and was performed by our instructor. I am forever grateful for that profound experience. It means something different when you write about what you've experienced as opposed to what you have studied.

The superconscious mind is that part of ourselves that houses the wisdom of the world. Unlike the conscious and subconscious minds, it can only act in our best interest, loving us unconditionally while constantly connected to Source energy. To me, this gift is the aspect of humanity that was made in the image of God. This is the part of us that knows the answers to the questions. To tap into this resource, a person just needs to be still and get to know and love that part of themselves that is Divine. With birth, I believe we forget this connection to the oneness of our existence. When people say this lifetime is a process of remembering who we are and how we are divinely created and connected, I believe the superconscious mind provides that avenue of opportunity. I am also convinced, through my experience, that we enter the world with energy or a set of beliefs or thought forms that predispose us to how our life's events unfold.

Meditation, when practiced regularly allows for the total and complete relaxation of the mind and body and places an individual in an altered state of consciousness that allows them to access the conscious, subconscious and superconscious minds—hence the statement, all the resources and answers can be found within. When a person gains access into their levels of consciousness there is no need to try to remember anything. The information a person seeks to gain will just come up into the awareness of the meditative mind.

Heart Centered Hypnotherapy, developed by Diane Zimberoff, M.A., is an incredible methodology to access the levels of consciousness and heal the self at many levels. Results of hypnotherapy sessions continue to demonstrate its effectiveness in healing the self of subconscious beliefs and patterns that sabotage our happiness and health of mind, body and spirit. I really believe the conscious mind can only heal to a certain extent, as it is missing vital information that can only be accessed through the subconscious mind. When past experiences are painful, my clients have been shown events of their childhood or youth on a video or TV screen. This allows them to *observe* instead of *relive* these events. It's less personal and painful and it becomes a safe option for their exploration into painful memories. I believe the higher wisdom of the self allows this. As painful memories of abuse are often placed into a vat of amnesia by a part of ourselves that protects, I believe the self also presents information when the time is right using a safe and acceptable methodology. Great clarity is often gained while the pain is minimized. While in the hypnotic trance, a person can develop new conclusions and affirmations to replace the conclusions drawn from the wounded child. Studies have substantiated that traditional psychotherapy often takes longer to see the kind of results experienced with hypnotherapy. My experience has been that a person needs to be ready and willing to partake in Hypnotherapy for it to be most effective.

Psych-K is also a methodology that has proven to be fruitful. As a Psych-K practitioner, I have witnessed people accessing files in their subconscious mind and re-wiring sabotaging beliefs. These issues are accessed in the subconscious mind using muscle testing or kinesiology, and are healed in conjunction with the conscious mind.

As leaders, it's important to understand the levels of consciousness because we are not only dealing with our own self-sabotaging beliefs; we're dealing with others', too. Many team dysfunctions are related to what is going on in the subconscious minds of its members. Triggers from childhood can be reactivated when one team member's words or actions remotely resemble and therefore harmonize with the defeat or hurt of the wounded child. The conscious mind may only know that it has been offended and it may be able to explain why but there may be deeper issues that only the subconscious mind can explain. Triggers during team meetings may fly frequently, causing internal and external disruptions in the harmony and effectiveness of the team. For the most part, we are conditioned to control our actions on the outside. In a leadership meeting, it's unlikely that a person will have a tantrum and throw themselves on the floor, while kicking their feet and yelling and screaming and crying. On the inside, however, we may or may not be conditioned to control our emotions and feelings. Some people hold things in until they explode. This explosion can be an outburst that is out of character for this person or it could be in the form of an illness. When we only scrape the surface of what can be analyzed at a conscious level, we limit our ability to extinguish painful emotions and feelings. Permanently healing situations will allow leaders to understand why their reactions are such and they will ultimately be a more productive team member and a happier person as a result of the inner work. I'm not suggesting that a leader mandate their subordinates to have hypnotherapy or any kind of therapy but I think awareness of the levels of consciousness and how they affect the prosperity of teams is important. Just an awareness of the possibilities can assist teams to function at a higher level of trust and harmony.

As we discussed before, a powerful tool is also the awareness and utilization of the collective consciousness of a workgroup, community, country, or planet. I'm a firm believer in the idea that "thoughts are things." Our visual perception, that which can be seen by the human eye, excludes so much of what is really around us in our environment. For example, to name just a few, with the naked eye, it is not humanly possible to see the frequencies that our radios, cell phones, TVs, and wireless internet pick-up in our environment. We know however, that these frequencies are there because we can turn on our radios, TVs, cell phones, and computers and see the results of these transmissions. In this case, the cause is invisible but the effect is visible. Thoughts work the same way. Cause occurs in the realm of the mind whereas effect occurs in the realm of form. Cause may be unseen, but effect is usually quite obvious. We have previously discussed the cascade of chemical reactions that occur in the body as a result of our thoughts. We can conclude that within the human body, the law of cause and effect is constantly and continually activated by the magnitude of thoughts that cruise through our mind. Can you imagine the volume of thoughts coming from all the people on the planet? Is it possible that all these invisible thoughts create visible effects?

The innocent and loving child that is raised to believe that war or conflict is an important and necessary part of life will integrate those thoughts into their being. Their thoughts and actions will reflect the complementary thoughts and actions of those around them and their communities will accept the tragedy of adversity and loss as commonplace. I think thoughts are things and we create the existence of which we believe. What do you think?

In the workplace, the collective consciousness of the people that comprise that workgroup will create the personality and characteristics of the organization. Attitudes are contagious. There is great power when minds come together for the good of the whole and it renders opportunities for the collective consciousness to create a work environment that the stakeholders desire. The stakeholders include the owners, leaders, employees and anybody else that provides the sweat equity to create and reap the rewards of the goods or services produced. If everyone on this planet could place love and peace, first for themselves and then for others at the top of their list of moment to moment thoughts, the world would be an entirely different place than it is today. Perhaps mother earth would even rejoice and who knows—maybe there would be less extreme and unusual weather patterns. I think it's possible for the energy of peace to be created by the collective thoughts of the inhabitants of this planet. In this scenario, the explosion and eruption of energy from the pressure cooker of adversity and ill thoughts would fade away.

A leader can tap into the collective consciousness of the people and use their energy to create and manifest positive outcomes when the desires are within the best interest of the whole. It's not so much about what is said, it's about what is thought. The intention and energy in our thoughts cannot be hidden from the knowing of the Universe. As Emerson said, "What you are shouts so loudly that I cannot hear what you say."

Within spiritual evolution, when the masses become aware that they can create their existence by recalling their divine nature and acknowledging the power of their individual and collective thoughts, a leader of this new world will function differently than most do today.

Chapter Seventeen

Patterns & Grooves

As James Brown said, "It's all in the groove." At one end of the spectrum, we can feel like we're in a groove that is so awesome we don't want it to end. At the other end of the spectrum, we can feel like we're in a groove that feels so awful it's as if a black cloud is hanging over our heads and following us everywhere we go. Sometimes we perceive ourselves to be stuck in a groove that completely lacks momentum but we can't seem to get moving up and out. At other times, the realization of being stuck in a groove may not surface to a level of awareness. The groove I'm referring to is created by recurrent patterns of thought, feelings or actions. These thoughts, feelings or actions act as triggers to create the neuro-network of chemical reactions we've discussed previously in this book. Recurrent patterns have a way of burning themselves into a groove with a hearty existence and sometimes it's very difficult to get rid of these habits. Through longevity and familiarity, these recurrent patterns continue to fire their cascade of reactors when triggered. The groove is a state of existence that we've created. Our life script unfolds because of the self-fulfilling prophesies we've written into the lines and margins. A self-fulfilling prophesy is an idea or theme or situation that we can see in the future and are convinced that's the way it will be, no matter what. At a conscious or unconscious level, everything we think and do will make it happen that way, whether it's in our best interest or not. If we believe we can, we will. If we believe we can't, we won't. We attract people and situations that most harmonize with our dominant thoughts. Like vibrations will attract like vibrations. When we fear something and focus on it, the energy we exude will attract the energy of that fear. If we continue to imagine a scenario and remain focused on this endpoint, everything we do will assist us in creating that scenario. If a person can identify that they're in a groove that no longer serves their well being, they can analyze the characteristics within that groove.

The first step in getting out of the groove is to recognize the groove exists. The second step is in gaining the awareness of why or how the groove came into existence.

People can analyze the major themes and patterns of recurrence in their life that gave birth to the groove. When life themes imprison people in the grooves they no longer desire to occupy, it is because those themes or patterns of thought continue to dominate their conscious choices and they believe they have no way out. People create their hindrances and are limited by the boundaries they place on themselves.

It is not uncommon to identify the same theme in many aspects of life. Nobody has to accept a theme as their "lot in life" as they can make choices to get away from the themes that bind and inhibit them. In the self-mastery journey, as our authenticity or true essence emerges from the grooves maintained by self-perceived limitations and false beliefs, we can acquire the ability to experience life the way we hope it can be. We have the potential to experience a life filled with love, hope and joy that allows our days to flow in an easier, more peaceful and fulfilling way. When we create a new direction for the current of which a happy and peaceful life flows, we can eventually ride that current with ease, even through rough waters. As with a broken record, we control how long the needle is caught in the groove—there are no victims and we have nobody to blame but ourselves.

In our humanness, patterns are a natural part of our existence. I sit in the same place at the dinner table every night. I sit in the same place at every board meeting. I drive the same route into work. Many of us are creatures of habit and although I may relish change in many aspects of my life, routines have always held a significant place in my life. I've always believed that consistency in certain aspects of life allows us the freedom to be flexible and adaptable in others. I have to live in a neat house. I can handle an abundance of stress at work but if I walk into a messy house, it sets me off into a whirlwind of aggravation and contention. Other people's clutter does not affect me, however, and I'm not bothered by what is comfortable to other people—as long as they don't live with me! Patterns influence and create our lives and understanding their existence leads us to question their value and how they affect our thoughts and create our world. Some we will want to change and others we won't. A good place to start is to evaluate the patterns in our lives that do not bring us joy.

There are many faces of fear that can be included in patterns of thought and action. Anger can act like a cancer that continues to grow until it finally impedes function. Living in habitual anger and/or resentment is like wearing a costume that disguises our appearance and hides the divine beauty that rests deeply in our hearts. Angry people may want to hide behind their mask, hiding themselves from people and maintaining an excuse to not face the reasons why they are so angry. Anger will eventually manifest in some level of discomfort up to and including dis-ease. Love is the most powerful remedy to extinguish anger. Chronic anger is a choice that serves to hurt the self.

Jealousy is another manifestation of fear that may reside within the self. There are many reasons why people are jealous but feelings of inadequacy, or of not being good enough may rest at the core of these emotions and feelings. When gratitude and love are consciously used to replace and heal feelings of inadequacy while looking deep within the self to understand how these feelings of lack were developed, remarkable progress to eliminate jealousy can be made.

Sadness is a choice. The roots of sadness need to be traced to their source to understand why that habit or choice of thought dominates. Perhaps at the core of all sadness is a human belief that we are separate from that which is divine and we believe outside influences compose, produce and direct our life's events. When we recognize and feel oneness within the core of our being, we understand that life is what it is because we made it that way. Every challenge, including those that foster sadness within us, has a greater purpose that yields evolution and growth. I have known many that blame other people, events and even God for the patterns that have and continue to manifest in their lives. Things are not always what they appear to be and perhaps a different perspective will illuminate a decision to be happy instead of sad.

Rejection is another manifestation of the root emotion of fear. A predilection to feelings of rejection is often developed in early childhood. The energy of rejection can subsequently be carried into adulthood, creating more opportunities for rejection. Characteristics of family life and how the child fits into that unit are often misunderstood by the undeveloped mind. Early conclusions and assumptions can foster feelings of rejection when the cause of events has nothing to do with the child. The knowing and memory of these events often reside outside conscious awareness but the memories remain vibrant in the subconscious mind. Regardless of the reasons and circumstances, the choice within the co-created plan to be exposed to opportunities should bring comfort in knowing that we placed the potential for those challenges in our path for a reason and at some level of consciousness, we know the reason. Ultimately, the reason is soul growth and spiritual evolution—for our growth and the growth of others.

Depression and anxiety are manifestations of fear that can be related to a plethora of reasons. The important fact here is knowing that we have a choice and we have the tools within to deal with many forms of depression and anxiety. Professional assistance is often helpful and sometimes paramount. When depression is caused by a chemical imbalance, treatment for this imbalance is as important as treatment for any other disorder, illness or disease.

All manifestations of fear have the potential to paralyze a person from decision making, being successful and just plain enjoying life. There are many people in leadership positions that are afraid to make decisions and take risks. They are often silently paralyzed because of the fears that plague them. Leaders can be blinded by their intelligence such that they can't see the role fear plays in their decision making. Their intelligence substantiates their paralysis in some analytical way using business terminology. Long term, the lack of decision making and risk taking because of fear can lead to the demise of an organization. Love can be the healer of fear.

Have you ever noticed that you can't be caught up in love and fear at the same time? Try it now. Think of something that makes you extremely angry or frustrated and try maintaining that feeling while you think of somebody or something you love. The Universal Law of Substitution states that two opposing thoughts cannot occur at the same time. I experienced this phenomenon, very early one morning when I was trying desperately to meditate upon a work related issue of which I needed clarity and direction. Regardless of how much I tried, I could not access any internal or divine information, clarity or wisdom. After what seemed like hours but was actually less than 15 minutes, I recognized that it was because I was so angry and filled with dislike for this company that was trying to interfere with patient care, my negative feelings were getting in my way. I could not access love based knowing and clarity, as anger and frustration were occupying my space. Before I could make any progress, I had to spend time eliminating anger and dislike by replacing it with love. I used two visual aids and performed a brief self-guided imagery *mediation*. One form of imagery was of our cancer patients. Although primarily nameless to me, they are our number one priority and they are a population of people who are easy to love and care about. The second was the people who worked for this company who were just pawns and had no ability to change an organizational culture. They were good people just doing their jobs. I had to visualize them at home with their families, having fun and being the good people I believed them to be. Love and fear cannot occupy the same space at the same time. Once the fear, in the form of anger and dislike was removed, I could clearly see optimal choices for resolution. Recalling that just days before at a staff meeting, I requested that each employee close their eyes and visual the endpoint of resolution and the formation of a partnership with this company, I was confident our combined energies and desire to render the best care would have a positive outcome. Within a couple of weeks, the issues were resolved in the best interest of our practice and patients. Two facts were substantiated for me. One was that love and fear cannot exist in the mind and heart at the same time and the other was the power of the collective consciousness of our work group.

It is important to identify the core emotions that create feelings within our bodies and identify where those feeling reside in the body. A conscious effort can be made to identify the discomfort and work on eliminating it from the mind and body. Deep breathing works wonders to minimize discomfort. Contemplation and meditation aimed at bringing clarity and rational thought to life is extremely valuable.

The manifestations of fear in our lives and in our work act as detours to success in an organization by paralyzing the sum of its parts. Using the power of thoughts we create our existence. With time and understanding of our divine selves, becoming impervious to the negative energy and actions of others is facilitated. It is essential to consistently put forth effort to protect ourselves from negativity that is released from others. Other people's stuff, if allowed, can form the sludge that seems to take residence within the crevices of one's consciousness. It is imperative to gain an understanding of what issue belongs to whom, as this sludge manifests wearing many disguises.

Within the complexities of life, the necessity for self-discipline and self-control appear nonnegotiable. They are imperative for a leader. When a member of a team feels threatened, their survival strategies are placed in overdrive and the core emotions embedded in the grooves and patterns of their life are activated. We can only take responsibility for ourselves and ownership of thoughts, emotions and actions need to reside with the person who created them, not the person who instigated them. Power is often given to others to instigate emotions within ourselves. People act as mirrors, reflecting those parts of ourselves that are in need of a brush-up.

Chapter Eighteen

Meditation = Graduation

Enlightenment and the evolution of soul are facilitated with a dedication to stillness. The journey is unique and without end. Each person needs to figure out what is best for them and develop their own path, unique to their needs and desires. There should be no judgment of the self or others. It is helpful to remember that everyone is at the perfect place in their evolution.

When the urge to move in one direction or another calls, a person should follow their hearts and instincts and proceed in the manner that resonates at their core and feels comfortable. The journey must be our own as what works for one person doesn't necessary work for another. Meditation is an excellent exercise to bring clarity of thought and reconnection of the mind, body and spirit. As mentioned previously, meditation is an effective method to alter the states of consciousness to access information and wisdom that has no boundaries of time and space.

Meditation has gotten a bad rap with some people because it is misunderstood. I don't mean people speak ill about it, I mean that people think they can't do it. Many think meditation is for the gurus and yogis or calm people who are really good at relaxing. They think their mind must be absent of any thought and their legs must be contorted in directions that are close to impossible. Some think they would need to set hours aside and others feel meditation is better left to others more suited to remain calm and relaxed.

Thinking myself a person with two basic speeds, fast and sleep, I never imagined I would be able to meditate. When I was a little girl, my Grandma always told me I couldn't sit still. It's not unusual to see me run, just because I don't want to waste time walking. I am known for aggravating my family and friends because I often shake tables and chairs while my body rocks or my legs swing or bop up and down. There was a time in my life when the thought of meditating never even entered my mind, as I thought it impossible for somebody like me.

When I began my CEO position with Hematology-Oncology Associates I was very interested in integrative medicine. Cancer patients were beginning to ask for complementary modalities such as Reiki, Healing Touch, Massage Therapy, Foot Reflexology and Acupuncture. To establish a program with these modalities required that I learn what they were and understand how they could be implemented into conventional therapy and the management of patient care. I was so overwhelmed with awe after my first Reiki session that my life was never to be the same. I was committed to assist in the development of an integrative/wellness program for our patients but I never imagined I would spend the next four years studying and preparing to become a Reiki Master/Teacher. I'm amazed and honored to say that I have taught this natural healing art to almost 20% of our workforce.

One day, shortly after I took my first Reiki class, as I would regularly practice balancing my energy centers or chakras, I thought, "If ever I were going to try to meditate, now could be the time." I seemed to be very calm inside and I had maintained a level of stillness for several minutes. Reiki provided my introduction into the world of meditation and today, I've added a new speed called "still and still awake." For me the gift initially was to be able to focus and continue to use my thoughts to concentrate on the color and rotation of the chakras. It allowed me to sit still, and although the activity in my mind was winding down, I was convinced that I was still being productive. Today, I can say I don't think I can meditate in any form close to a Yogi, although I don't really know exactly what that form is, but what I can say is that it works for me and the results of the last 10 years of meditation have made a significant and substantial difference in my life. I have come to understand elements of myself that I may have never had the time and focus to explore. I am able to communicate with the part of myself that lends powerful insight, information and healing. My intuition has catapulted to levels I would not have believed possible for myself years ago. The best is that I know, I've only just begun and my life will continue to provide me with insights and wisdom that will surprise and fulfill me. Every day is a new opportunity.

I have as busy a life as anybody else and I find time for this stillness because it's a priority for me. I have come to understand, however, that one of my misunderstandings was that meditation must occur while the body is motionless. I have developed a 30—40 minute moving meditation exercise that I would like to share. Most mornings, I get on my treadmill and while I'm getting my cardiac exercise, my mind is in one of "my" states of altered consciousness. Perhaps my definition of meditation during this session is unique, but it works for me and may work for others, especially the busy personalities that don't think meditation is an option for them. I think because of my personality and the unique and individual journey that all of us take in an attempt to achieve peace and knowing, I created a time to meditate that combined physical exercise with chakra balancing, chakra alignment, and guided imagery. I'm a good multi-tasker and why should the evolution of my consciousness not be advantaged by that personality trait? When I do this exercise, I feel like my mind is separate from the motions of my body. I feel that somehow, within the motion there is stillness at the core. It sounds weird but it really works for me. For those that may be interested in attempting this moving meditation or for those who are perhaps just curious, I offer a potential daily routine.

The treadmill session is performed with closed eyes. At first this posed a challenge to me, but after I got accustomed to hanging on while walking fast on the treadmill, any fear of falling off or imbalance ceased. As an aside, I have to say this was also an excellent exercise in recognizing fear, feeling it and releasing it. I paid a great deal of attention to how the fear arose and maintained itself in my body while I was fearful to fall off the treadmill. It was a good indicator for me because it was an obvious feeling and I knew why and where the fear originated. The release of this fear provided insights as to how I could use this awareness in my daily life. (OK—back to the moving mediation exercise.) The highest inclination is set at the beginning of the mind/body workout and it is decreased over time throughout the session, in increments that one desires. I found the speed that was best for me to ultimately finish the session while burning the number calories I desired. In addition, my goal was to find the fastest speed that would not interfere with my moving meditation by causing my mind to wander due to *fall-off* anxiety.

My routine has evolved in many ways over the years, but here's the summary of how it began. If you're interested, just use your intuition to develop your unique moving meditation. The first 10–15 minutes are spent in contemplation and review of recent events or concerns. Whatever bothered me, whether it was people or situations or challenges of any kind, my first goal was to remove them from my head and energy field. Hence the first mind-exercise was a vortex of light that would come from the heavens, fill and consume the

Crown Chakra (imagining a ball or star of bright white light about 6-8 inches above the head), and begin to penetrate the spine in a column of bright, divine, healing, white light. This column would slowly get wider and wider until it formed a vortex of light. The vortex would then spin and as it did, heal and protect my energy fields from any disruption that did not serve my highest good. This vortex would then remove any issues that were bothering me from my field, by catching them in the vortex of divine light and whisking them away. We often carry burdens that don't belong to us. We carry them out of love, thinking that it assists the people we love. These challenges, however, are always in the highest good of those to whom they belong. They are not for anybody to carry but the owner. The owner of these burdens needs to work though them, overcome them and grow from the adversity. I visualized the vortex healing relationships by removing anyone's personal clutter that may have lodged in my field. I visualized the clutter coming from any person who I was giving the power to alter my emotions and level of inner peace and harmony. I visualized situations or challenges of which I could not change, remove or solve and therefore served no purpose to remain in my energy fields. Acceptance of these situations therefore became the objective. Accept what you can't change and move on with a positive attitude. During this light vortex exercise, white light was often dusted with egoic particles or debris that turned the white light gray, but as it spun and cleansed and healed, the brightness and whiteness returned. The time of the vortex exercise would vary but intuitively, I would know when it was complete. Upon completion, I felt so much better. The exercise made me feel lighter and brighter and more connected to the positive nature and beauty of life. I was ready to start my day fresh, cleansed from anything that bothered me. I felt protected by the white light that would surround me throughout my day, acting as an impervious shield, pillar or column of protection from negative thought forms or negative vibes of any kind.

When my field was cleansed, I moved on to the balancing of the energy centers or seven major chakras in the body. In Chapter Nine, I explained the colors and locations of the major chakras. I visualized the color and rotation of the chakras (they usually rotate clockwise, as if your face was the clock, and the colors from the base up are red, orange, yellow, green, blue, indigo/violet and white). When my field was cleansed and my chakras balanced, I would breath and bath myself in white light. I would then still my mind, breathe and feel immersed in this divine light, emanating from the heavens. By this time, the elevation of the treadmill was usually flat and I would just walk and concentrate on my breath and the vibration of perfection that was occurring in every cell in my body. The session gave me a feeling of vibrating with the divine light, in the oneness of all existence. I continued to bath myself in white, pure, divine light until I intuitively knew the session was complete and it was time to close. Periodically, I opened my eyes to check the time and calories burned while on the treadmill. I always walk off the treadmill in a much better state than I get on.

There are other light exercises that I've integrated, as I've been doing this for many years, but this information should be sufficient to get anyone started. For me, I sweat a lot, get a good workout and feel like I'm able to overcome any challenges of the day before they begin. After the treadmill, I do other exercises and some yoga. At the completion of all exercises, I do a 3–5 minute still meditation, sitting with legs crossed. During that short time, I *still* everything I can while focusing on the breath. I am amazed at how wonderful I always feel after a morning session. It's that knowing of how I feel after exercise that helps me to continue doing it, especially on the days when extra sleep would be preferred.

Everyone's path is different and perfect. I offer this information solely because it works for me and perhaps those people, who watch TV or listen to music while exercising, may want to try this and use their imagination to pass the time, instead. I have known many people that need to unwind and release from the tensions of the day. Since I'm a passionate proponent of prevention, I like to clear the field, and strengthen my fortitude before my day. I'd rather be impervious to most of life's crap than have to scrap it off.

As with everyone, a leader has voluminous opportunities throughout their workday to become aggravated, frustrated, exhausted and more. A healthy start to any day should include exercise and good nutrition for the body, mind, and spirit. Meditation is a great way to protect the integrity of the mind and fortify resilience. It offers opportunities for clarity and for enriching self-love and the love of everything and everyone.

Chapter Nineteen

The Fruits of your Labors & the Season of Harvest

The concepts presented in this book weave together to form a workable and achievable canvas of love and productivity in life and the workplace. The world will become a loving, peaceful environment when its inhabitants put forth the love and sincerity to work from the inside-out, healing the mind, body and spirit and creating an atmosphere of oneness. When a loving and forgiving and grateful collective consciousness reaches saturation, peace and love will abound.

The foundation of a successful leader is love. Love of self, love of people and love of leadership. When fear is replaced with love, success knows no boundaries. As more people stray from organized religion, opportunities to share gifts of time and treasure that religious communities commonly provided can be replaced by workplace communities. Stewardship becomes the best insurance policy of which an organization can partake, as it is in giving that we receive. When quality, service, love, gratitude and stewardship pour out of an organization, the Universe will ensure it receives the abundance it gives. The workplace can become the community of people that come together to share their gifts of stewardship. The support of worthy foundations through the giving of time and money will in return, bring loving energy to a workgroup. The satisfaction of helping those less fortunate and the fulfillment of giving assists in bringing a workgroup together for a common good and offers great opportunities for bonding. Friendships are forged and maintained and opportunities for laughter and fulfillment become treasured memories. Stewardship in the workplace can provide a network of thought to create the type of organization that will be successful in our future. The collective consciousness of the whole can create the existence desired to support and foster a culture of mastery. Self-mastery in the workplace will encourage and produce the greatest self-fulfilling prophesy of any organization—we can do anything and be anything we desire.

There are ways to create a culture of accountability where the journey of self-mastery is encouraged and facilitated. The self-mastery journey requires a commitment to the mind-body-spirit of the most valuable assets of an organization—the employees. I have mentioned several ideas throughout this book and provide the following as ideas or reminders.

A leader needs to be creative or at least resourceful to figure out ways to keep their workforce balanced. Having committees to work on this is a viable option. A wellness co-coordinator and committee can develop fun ways to help the group stay healthy and balanced. There are many creative ways to unite a workforce while encouraging healthy lifestyles. A committee (we call it the Fun Committee) can be established that represents a cross section of all departments whose purpose is to orchestrate events that unify an organization and assist the community through charitable giving of time, talent and treasure. It's a great idea to offer classes like Yoga, Pilates, Zumba and meditation. There are all sorts of ways to assist a work group to feel appreciated and unified. We also have two leaders trained in a program called "TRP." It stands for the "Totally Responsible Person" and it's a program that supports many of the ideas presented in this book. There is training available for key personnel and a program established for these philosophies to be shared with employees to assist in building a culture of cooperation and accountability. As I mentioned previously, it's important to offer an EAP—Employee Assistance Program as a benefit to each employee. These professionals can provide counseling for both personal and professional issues. For larger organizations that can support the efforts of a social worker, I think it behooves an organization to have this psychosocial assistance on site. I would love to see a discipline of social work developed for organizational development through self-mastery. The 360 evaluation also helps to create a culture of accountability because everyone an employee comes in contact with on a daily basis can have an opportunity to evaluate the contribution that person makes to the organization. My idea was the 8 ½ x 11, a word to provoke thought at each monthly staff meeting that promotes harmony and self-mastery. There are many ways for a leader to foster self-mastery in the work place. As the vibration of one person increases, it increases the whole. This elevates the collective consciousness of the workgroup to a higher level of love based thoughts.

As the self-mastery journey takes form in the hearts and minds of individuals, it will transcend to the workplace and those characteristics articulated at the start of this book will come to fruition. The fruits of the labors of self-love will be many and will harmonize a workplace in ways that exceed most leaders' expectations. I feel it's worth repeating the characteristics of an evolved organization, especially since the words should be flavored by a new perspective that has been conveyed within these pages.

- A good, healthy morale will be maintained
- The work force will demonstrate a higher level of job satisfaction and effectiveness
- There will be greater harmony within work groups and among the organization
- There are less supervisors and managers and more leaders
- Leadership will spend less time with drama within their teams
- Leadership will spend less time with drama within the organization
- New ideas will be sprouting up on a routine basis and people will be taking more stock in their levels of accountability
- There will be a general feeling that people care and the staff will be productive
- Efficiency will improve and more people will want to be involved in process improvement because they will feel like a stake holder
- Unique and customary challenges are dealt with in a more positive manner and adverse outcomes have a shorter duration
- Stewardship becomes more visible within the organization and a commitment to community is broadened
- An organization begins to function in a similar fashion to a sacred community to help others, especially fellow team members, who are less fortunate or who experience extraordinarily difficult circumstances
- Staff unites their efforts in more global ways to improve or enrich the lives of others—what they give will come back a thousand fold or more
- Indices of financial success improve and more time is spent acting than worrying
- The "air" is lighter and filled with fulfillment and joy
- Customer/Client satisfaction is high and everyone is treated with respect and dignity
- The organization becomes an employer of choice
- The organization becomes a provider/supplier of choice

Chapter Twenty

Making the world a better place, one person at a time, from the inside-out

Self-mastery can only occur from the inside-out. Inquire within for the strongest, most loving resources available to mankind. Spirituality is enriched by having a knowing of what spirituality is, by having a basic understanding of what it sounds and feels like, and most importantly, by immersion. Immersing the self in love and love filled activities. Immersing the self in opportunities to feel gratitude and a connection to nature and people enriches spirituality. Immersing ourselves in opportunities to forgive will enrich the path. Loving and trusting the self with a complete heart and soul creates a new world that begins to form within, the reflection of which is a light to the world. Twelve, "8½ x 11" snippets follow—I have included a brief guided imagery or meditation with each to enrich the experience of the word. You may use these guided meditations, segments of the meditations or you can create your own. I have included 12 with the suggestion that one word be contemplated or meditated upon each month. I encourage you to develop your own affirmations to augment this experience and repeat them before and after each exercise.

You may ask, why would a book about leadership have guided meditations in it? I would ask, how could it not? Being a great leader requires a ton of effort and consumes a lot of energy. If we don't learn how to replenish our spirits, over time, the void will cause discomfort. Overtime, the discomfort can cause burn-out or even dis-ease. Be kind to yourself for all you give in a day. If you don't replenish, there won't be more to give. You deserve all the gifts life can offer. You may find the meditations more effective if you digitally record them and listen with your headphones. Don't worry—even if you're big and strong . . . very important and successful . . . even if you make tons of money . . . nobody will know you've decided to relinquish the control, open your heart and meditate. Just try it!

In the words of the Chinese philosopher, Lao Tzu, "Truly the greatest gift you can give is that or your own self-transformation."

8½ x 11s

Sincerity

We begin our 8 ½ x 11s with the word sincerity. Sincerity is an embodiment of true love and is the most important element that must be present for the self-mastery journey to commence and continue. Without a sincere desire for self-realization, a person proceeds through the motions without a true willingness to put forth the effort to evolve. A sincere desire to look within and evolve must be present for the journey to have meaning and be successful. Academic achievement requires effort and hard work. Self-mastery and spiritual growth requires patience, sincerity and interest. Sincerity fosters a greater awareness and allows the conditions within the self to be ripe for self-mastery. Relax, open your heart and be sincerely interested in the evolution of the self. When we interact with each other with genuine sincerity, we see the beauty and divinity within each of us and tend to ignore the faults and frailties. Immerse yourself in sincere dedication to remembering the divinity within the self and practice self-mastery with sincere intent to love. Your affirmations may include: I am sincere in my desire to understand myself; I sincerely love myself; I am sincere in my love for others.

*

Sit in a comfortable position and breathe in and out a few times with your eyes closed. Just relax and feel the tension release from every part of your body from your toes to your head. Think about your life's journey and how you have overcome so many challenges. Congratulate yourself for taking the time to just sit and relax. Meditate on the journey of self-mastery where you'll take great care to enter the recesses of your mind and body to understand where you've been and where you're going, knowing that you are in control of your life and have a great power and mystery within.

Picture a beautiful clear lake in which all the debris of life has settled to the bottom. Make a commitment to yourself to stir the waters of your existence such that the newly suspended particles can be identified and cleared without fear or anxiety. Meditate on a life that takes on ease because all challenges become opportunities where love energy and divine clarity permeate your existence. See yourself as a child and watch yourself grow to who you are today. Give thanks for all the challenges that got you to where you are and feel the immense love in your heart for yourself. Meditate and feel the sincerity in your heart to master who you are—have confidence that every tool you need is right inside yourself. Breathe and feel the sincerity in your heart to love and understand yourself—to forgive yourself for any faults or errors in judgment and to unite your human self with its divine counterpart. With a feeling of complete sincerity, commit to embark on a path of self-discovery, self-love and self-mastery. Within this meditation, let there be space between your thoughts and allow the space to get bigger and bigger, setting your mind and true-self free while taking time to enjoy the expanse of inner-peace and clarity.

Make a commitment to yourself to be sincere in your desire to commit the time and energy to understand your core beliefs—those that reside beneath the birthplace of your perceptions. Relax, open your heart and be sincerely interested in the evolution of self. Know that spiritual growth just requires sincerity, an open mind, a readiness to absorb the new and shed the limitations of the past. In our sincerity we will attract that which we seek—for we will have sincere intent.

Picture yourself surrounded by an egg shaped white light with flecks of gold and silver, shimmering with love. Allow this light to envelop your body and extend into your energy fields about 3 feet away from you. Breathe in the light and just sit and relax, bathed in this love, and when your mind wanders, just bring it back to your breath and the light. When you feel complete, begin to feel the physical body and bring yourself back to your physical environment. Open your eyes and see a world that is brightened by the love you exude from your heart.

Love

Love is one of the most meaningful and important words in the treasury of language. Self-mastery cannot be contemplated or journeyed until love of self flows from the deepest recesses of our soul through every organ and tissue and exudes from every pore of our being. It is then that love can extend to others and an appreciation for the beauty and abundance of our Universe can be experienced and shared. With love comes gratitude, as love shines its light on the magnificence of our existence, our hearts cannot help but overflow with complete and sincere gratitude.

So many metaphors in prose and poetry have been put to paper in an attempt to define the indefinable, to articulate the un-articulateable, to explain the unexplainable. The experience of love, however, is unmistakable and when present, is always known. The illusion of love, however, can be disappointing. The illusion that we believe to be real love that comes with conditions and expectations can sadden and disappoint. What is thought to be love may be a derivative of the self reaching out to heal a core belief of lack. Some may possess a core belief that they are not good enough –that they are not worthy of love or happiness. When these beliefs exist they will attract more of the conditions that created them. As we begin to acknowledge the perfect spirit that resides within ourselves, we begin to love and accept our divinity. All we seek to love can be found within the recesses of our hearts and minds. With self-love comes the love of all.

As the love cycle gains more frequent repetitions and greater girth, life takes on new dimensions of fulfillment. Relationships prosper; service to others becomes an insatiable desire and nature takes on an everlasting and more magnificent beauty than ever before. Flowers will even speak to the soul. An overwhelming beauty and flavor engulfs each breath and love resonates from every corner of existence.

Love—the vibration of perfection, the vibration of God made manifest. Difficult to explain but the knowing is never mistaken. Your affirmations may include: I am love; I am light; I am divine; I am.

*

Sit quietly, in a comfortable position, close your eyes, breathe and begin to relax. Feel your body going deeper and deeper into relaxation. Breathe the breath of life, the gift that allows us to be human and be filled with love and life. Breathe and relax, letting all the anxieties, worries and burdens melt and fall off like snow from the roof on a warm, sunny day.

Allow a picture to develop in your mind of a person you love so very, very much. See that person, watch them smile and laugh and be filled with happiness. Allow the love you feel for this person to swell your heart. Picture the love filling your heart and spilling over, like a cup runneth over, permeating every cell in your body. Allow your body to become love. Take pause to feel what that love feels like. Pay attention to how the cells in your body are reacting to this love. Feel the love saturate your being such that you feel like you're bursting with the emotion of love. Feel the love in your body and continue to breathe, breathe, breathe. If your mind wanders, bring your attention back to the breath and the feeling of love that permeates every cell in your body.

Bring your attention back to the picture of the person you love and allow another person, place or thing that you truly love to take shape in the next picture. Repeat the love exercise explained above as many times as you'd like, enriching the love experience more and more with each guided imagery. When you're ready to move on to the next image, as you are filled with this love experience, picture yourself as a child, wide-eyed and ready to explore and greet the world with love and without judgment. Continue to visualize yourself grow into the person you are today, and continue to send love and feel love for that beautiful soul. Feel that love of self and allow the love to deepen and cement itself into the crevices of your mind, body and spirit.

When you have completed the love exercises, allow that love to linger and make a commitment to yourself to work on having these loving feelings throughout the day. The more often these love exercises are performed, the more deeply this feeling of love becomes baked and integrated into your being. With practice, you will be able to return to this place of love in your heart at a moments notice. With intention, know that when life gets difficult or frustrating, you can immediately return to the feeling of love in your heart to sooth and nurture and fortify yourself to become impervious to negativity, as love protects and guides. Allow loving yourself and others to become the habit that directs your thoughts and deeds.

In closing, allow yourself to be surrounded by an egg shaped white light with flecks of gold and silver, shimmering with love. Allow this light to envelop your body and extend into your energy fields about 3 feet away from you. Breathe in the light and just sit and relax, bathed in this love, and when your mind wanders, just bring it back to your breath and the light. When you feel complete, begin to feel the physical body and bring yourself back to your physical environment. Open your eyes and see a world that is brightened by the love you exude from your heart.

Perception

Perceptions are the interpretations of how we view and understand life as we process the incoming sensations of sight, sound, smell, touch, taste and intuition. How and why we perceive life the way we do is complex and related to a magnitude of variables. Regardless of how we perceive life, our perception becomes our reality. At times, we distort the incoming stimuli to fit into the illusions of life that we have created and feel comfortable in living. Perceptions may vary from individual to individual but the fact that a person's perception becomes their reality remains constant.

There is much in life that we perceive to be true so we believe that it's true and we therefore act like it's true. Religion and politics are two topics that offer many opportunities to create perceptions that foster personal and group beliefs and corresponding actions. Our perceptions influence the life we create. We perceive life as it's filtered through the lens created from our life's experiences, both consciously and unconsciously, to view life. The internal language of communication that is created when events or stimuli pass through this lens is called self-talk. We engage in self-talk most of our conscious life. Self-talk makes up the sentences and paragraphs of our autobiography. Self-talk describes life as it is interpreted from the lens of which we view the world.

Our self-directed thoughts and perceptions create happiness and joy as well as anger, resentment and sadness. When self-talk is accurate and rational, people function well. When self-talk is irrational and untrue, chaos and dysfunction in created. When a person perceives that "stuff" is happening to them, instead of just happening, they enter the domain of stress. How often do you think events are happening to you, instead of just happening in the random order of life's creations? Your affirmations may include: I am love; I am abundance.

*

Sit quietly, in a comfortable position, close your eyes and breathe and begin to relax. Feel your body going deeper and deeper into relaxation. Breathe in the breath of divine light and feel the light penetrate your body. Feel the white light around you, filling your lungs and bringing the healing vibration of perfection to all cells of the body. Breathe and relax, releasing all the anxieties, frustrations and stresses of the day. Begin at your feet and focus on every area, allowing each muscle in your body to release tension and relax. Picture a beautiful angel with a large white basket coming into view. With a loving smile she desires that you place all your worries and troubles in that basket for her to whisk away to be handled by divine forces. You relinquish all doubts and toss all the issues bothering you into her basket. She nods a loving gaze of thanks and you watch her walk away and disappear into the light.

You are feeling a sense of incredible peace now and you are relaxed and still. Visualize our beautiful and abundant planet as though you were suspended in space. As you get closer and closer to the earth, you enter the atmosphere and begin to see the beautiful blue sky, clouds, water and landforms. As you are flying among the clouds, you see a large screen where different scenes are passing. You see an older woman who is crying. You are about to feel saddened by her tears but then you are shown that her tears are those of joy and love. You feel love for this woman, though she remains nameless. You send love to her and all those who cry tears of sadness or joy. The next scene that presents is that of children, running in the rain. The rain is coming down hard and at first, you think perhaps you should be concerned as to the safety and well-being of these children. Before your feelings can emote, you are shown that the children are running with great excitement, as the area had been in a dangerous time of draught and if rain did not come, there could have been significant challenges for the people. Your heart is exhilarated and you share in their joy and the child within begins to remember how much fun it was to run in the rain, so excited without worry or concern. The next scene you are shown is that of thousands and thousands of people walking in the dusk with candles lit and tears in their eyes, walking slowly and methodically. Your initial thought may be that they are walking in sympathy for some great loss, but you are soon shown that the event is a peace movement where civil discord had finally and permanently ceased and the inhabitants of the area are demonstrating their solidarity in peace and love. They are celebrating the end to fighting and war. Mothers and fathers are overcome with emotion knowing their sons and daughters will no longer be put in harm's way. You feel incredible love for these people and for their release of fear and the embrace of freedom and peace. You are filled with love for our abundant planet and all the people who live on it. You send light from your heart to blanket the world in love and peace and you feel such joy to be a part of this planet.

You are now back in your chair, still immersed in the light. You wonder why human nature so often jumps to negative and fearful conclusions, instead of jumping into a positive scenario first. You contemplate times in your life when you were certain your perceptions were correct but they were not.

You now fill your heart with love and light and make a commitment to maintain an open mind and think positive thoughts. You make a commitment to yourself to not judge yourself and be gentle, kind and loving of the self. You are filled with love and joy and you continue to sit in peace and light. You decide that your glass is always half full, never half empty.

In closing, allow yourself to be surrounded by an egg shaped white light with flecks of gold and silver, shimmering with love. Allow this light to envelop your body and extend into your energy fields about 3 feet away from you. Breathe in the light and just sit and relax, bathed in this love, and when your mind wanders, just bring it back to your breath and the light. When you feel complete, begin to feel the physical body and bring yourself back to your physical environment. Open your eyes and see a world that is brightened by the love you exude from your heart.

Patterns

Patterns are ubiquitous in nature as well in the minds and actions of people. As we look around, outside of ourselves, patterns can be noted everywhere. From the fashions we wear and carry, colors of which we surround ourselves, houses in which we live, buildings in which we work, churches in which we worship, stores in which we shop, roads of which we travel, board rooms in which we meet, doctors' offices in which we seek medical care, skyscrapers of which we marvel—to the beauty of nature with the magnitude of patterns of beauty that color our world, light our sky, and beautify our existence—patterns are everywhere.

Let us consider our patterns of thought. The patterns of thought that render the feelings and emotions that control our lives and permeate our existence. An analysis of our thought patterns that affect our physical, emotional, mental and spiritual lives, can help us to outline and analyze those patterns which no longer serve our highest good and the highest good of others and nature. How do the patterns of frustration, stress, anger, resentment, jealousy, judgment, disappointment and lack manifest in your life? Many of us, being creatures of habit, take comfort in the patterns of life. Some become complacent and accept patterns of thought and action because they do not want to expend the energy to change. Patterns of thought often repel the benefits of life we desire.

When we take time out of our busy schedules to contemplate the patterns of thought that mold our actions, we become mindful of those thoughts and activities that don't serve us. Awareness is the first step in healing. When we are controlled by our thought patterns, we become hostages to conscious and unconscious impulses. As we progress through our day let us observe our senses to see what attracts us and what repels us. This effort helps us gain mastery over our reactions and allows us to learn how to better manage our moods and emotions. Your affirmations may include: I have every tool I need to modify the patterns that no longer serve my highest good; I am love; I make healthy choices for myself.

*

Sit quietly, in a comfortable position, close your eyes and breathe and begin to relax. Feel your body going deeper and deeper into relaxation. Breathe in the breath of divine light and feel the light penetrate your body. Feel the white light around you, filling your lungs and bringing the healing vibration of perfection to all cells of the body. Breathe and relax, releasing all the anxieties, frustrations and stresses of the day. Begin at your feet and focus on every area, allowing each muscle in your body to release tension and relax. Continue to relax and become conscious of your breathing. Begin to consider the patterns that surround your life. Perhaps you can start with the obvious like picturing the patterns in your home furnishings, your dining habits, your hobbies or favorite vacation spots. When you are ready, venture within the sacred space of your mind and heart and as an observer, review some of your common thought patterns and reactions to given situations. As an observer, contemplate how you face disappointment, deal with stress and solve problems. Examine the drama in your life that causes discomfort and ask yourself to identify the patterns of thought that lead up to feelings and emotions that draw you into that drama. Tackle one type of drama at a time by thinking of how you can use your gift of choice to sever the process where thoughts are born or where they meet feelings. By having awareness of a pattern, you can break it. Work from the result you wish to have—visualize the outcome of any given situation and work backwards to the thoughts that will render the feelings and emotions to create that which you imagine anew. What thoughts and feelings will manifest your new outcome? Give thanks as though you have received what you seek and desire. Continue to meditate upon this new pattern of thought with gratitude. In time, you will recognize the old thought upon its birth and modify it immediately to signal the feelings and emotions that will result in your desired outcome. Know that as patterns of love and gratitude are plentiful, life takes on a greater ease and burdens seem to melt away like the old thoughts that formed them in the first place.

Let the patterns of love, gratitude, forgiveness, and tolerance become the basic ingredients of your thoughts. Know that internal patterns of thought create the external patterns of our existence. Where there is inner peace there will be outer peace.

In closing, allow yourself to be surrounded by an egg shaped white light with flecks of gold and silver, shimmering with love. Allow this light to envelop your body and extend into your energy fields about 3 feet away from you. Breathe in the light and just sit and relax, bathed in this love, and when your mind wanders, just bring it back to your breath and the light. When you feel complete, begin to feel the physical body and bring yourself back to your physical environment. Open your eyes and see a world that is brightened by the love you exude from your heart.

Form

Time offers a continuum of changing forms. Physically, emotionally, mentally and spiritually, the forms that create our bodies change. With time, thoughts, emotions, and relationships evolve and change form. The concept of the changing forms of life can be embraced and celebrated or foster fear and inadequacy. The concept that the forms of life are in continual alteration is neither good nor bad, it's just how it is, and acceptance is key to sustaining a healthy outlook on life during times of change.

The changing forms of relationships are a prime example of how the forms of life change. When love partnerships first begin, the relationship is passionate and there is so much to talk about and there is so much of the world to see together with a new, combined sight. As the years pass, the form of a partnership changes and evolves. Perhaps the passion is not as intense but the love deepens and a different level of togetherness evolves. As the years pass, perhaps companionship becomes most important, as there may be less excitement and new things to talk about but the familiarity and history provide great fulfillment and comfort.

The physical body undergoes many changes of form throughout life until the ultimate change in form when we transition out of our physical body into the realm of spirit. The essence of who we are remains and the energy of love is never exhausted. Death does not exist; it is merely an alteration of form. We never lose the people we love—they are but a breath away.

Take time to recognize and contemplate the changing forms of life. How do you view the changing of forms and how readily do you accept and embrace change? Your affirmations may include: I accept the forms of life with love and gratitude; I am open to change; I view all challenges as opportunities.

*

Sit quietly, in a comfortable position, close your eyes and breathe and begin to relax. Feel your body going deeper and deeper into relaxation. Breathe in the breath of divine light and feel the light penetrate your body. Feel the white light around you, filling your lungs and bringing the healing vibration of perfection to all cells of the body. Breathe and relax, releasing all the anxieties, frustrations and stresses of the day. Begin at your feet and focus on every area, allowing each muscle in your body to release tension and relax. Continue to relax and become conscious of your breathing. Begin to consider the many changes in form that life has offered. Celebrate your resiliency to accept the changes in form of which you have no control. Fill your heart with love for yourself and others and the changing vibrancy of the world around you.

Picture yourself in a beautiful garden. As you walk in this garden your senses are awakened to the absolute beauty that surrounds you. You see the beautiful blue sky with its billowy clouds. You can smell the scent of fresh air as the gentle breeze caresses your face and body. It is warm and sunny and the bright sun allows warmth to penetrate the cells of your body with a vibrancy of light that possesses an abundance of unconditional love that fills your heart with joy. As you walk in your special garden, you notice all the trees and flowers and beautiful sights. The beauty of nature fills your heart with such love for the abundance of the Universe and you feel a sense of gratitude that is more powerful than ever before. You hear the beautiful sounds of the birds singing the praises of the world. You feel united with all of nature and you recognize that you're not separate but you are connected to everything around you.

Take time to notice every aspect of this garden. Allow the love and beauty to fill you with love and gratitude. As you continue to explore your garden, you come across a lovely bench. You decide to sit on the bench and spend some time in stillness. Sit on the bench and continue to breathe in the light of life. When your mind wanders, just bring your attention back to the breath. Remain in this loving state for however long you desire. When you are ready, you walk back through the garden and come back to your physical awareness in the room of which you're seated. When it is time, open your eyes, feeling refreshed and excited to continue on your journey of life, knowing that you can always spend time in your special garden, whenever you wish. If life stresses you out, take a moment to be still and imagine your special garden. The sun always shines there and love is boundless.

Alignment

The alignment of which I speak is the alignment within the self that provides a knowing between the sacred space that represents our highest good and our life's plan and the space that we perceive to inhabit within the genres of our life. When we are in alignment, we possess a knowing that we are in the right place in all aspects of our life. This doesn't mean that we don't and won't have chaos and challenges but it does means that we have an inner peace in spite of the chaos and challenges because we know we are where we are supposed to be at this time in our life. When we feel out of alignment, our thoughts and actions that steer our choices from one space to another can be analyzed and modified. We always have a choice and we make choices at every junction throughout the day. Some choices are in our highest good and others do not serve us well. The good news is that we can love ourselves, be kind to ourselves and cut ourselves enough slack to develop a plan of action or correction to re-align with that which serves our highest good and brings love, peace and abundance to our lives. Contemplate the feeling of alignment within the different aspects of your life—relationships, careers, jobs, location, house, goals, etc. Contemplate your physical alignment, personal alignment, professional alignment, and spiritual alignment. Take note of where you feel the alignment when you contemplate one particular aspect of your life and determine whether it brings you feelings of comfort or discomfort. Where in your body do you feel these emotions and feelings? Where there is discomfort, send love and know that you have all the tools you need inside to make healthy choices for a life lived in love and joy. As we become receptive to a deeper level of self-trust, the quality of our choices are enhanced because of the wisdom that is offered through that self-love and trust. One of the greatest gifts we can give ourselves is to be guided by our authentic inner knowing and not follow someone else's recipe for life. Your affirmations may include: I align with my highest good; I am aligned with the light and love of the Universe; I follow my intuition and make my own decisions that are best for me.

*

Sit quietly, in a comfortable position, close your eyes and breathe and begin to relax. Feel your body going deeper and deeper into relaxation. Breathe in the breath of divine light and feel the light penetrate your body. Feel the white light around you, filling your lungs and bringing the healing vibration of perfection to all cells of the body. Breathe and relax, releasing all the anxieties, frustrations and stresses of the day. Begin at your feet and focus on every area, allowing each muscle in your body to release tension and relax. Continue to relax and become conscious of your breathing.

Become an observer and review the video screen of the major choices in your life, knowing that everything is always perfect in the oneness of our existence. Celebrate with yourself, those choices that you feel were healthy and consistent with your highest good. Smile inside and allow the love and pride to flow throughout your body.

Now, allow yourself to recognize the choices you perceive manifested in less than optimal outcomes. Things are not always what they appear to be, and slowly erase any negative feelings and replace them with love and pride for making the best choices at the time. Know that there was a greater purpose and a reason for any trials or tribulations that resulted from these choices and you would not have grown to be the person you are if they did not occur. Swell your heart with love for yourself. Watch yourself on the screen as you deal with any disappointments and send love to that person who is perfect and divine. Know that you have evolved because of the challenges, not because of the easy roads.

Now see the light of the Universe come down from the heavens and enter your crown chakra, the bright star located about 6—8 inches above your head. Allow that light to form a white, glowing rod that envelops your spine. See the alignment of that light in perfection. You may feel your shoulders rise and your spine begin to straighten. Know that you aligned with the oneness in perfect harmony. Your higher self, your divine self is always present to make healthy choices. Congratulate yourself for this awareness.

Allow that light to sooth your body and penetrate every cell. Bath in this unconditional loving light and feel a level of healing not known before in your body. Allow love to permeate all your cells and continue to breathe the light, with confidence and knowing that you have the ability and wisdom to create the life you want. You deserve to be happy. You are worthy of happiness.

Breathe in the light and just sit and relax, bathed in this love, and when your mind wanders, just bring it back to your breath and the light. When you feel complete, begin to feel the physical body and bring yourself back to your physical environment. Open your eyes and see a world that is brightened by the love you exude from your heart.

Magnet

Our thoughts are the magnets that attract the energy of likeness. Our life and ongoing creation of our existence are manifestations of the thoughts that permeate the Universe. The law of attraction states that we attract people and situations that most resonate with our dominant thoughts. The law of belief states that what you believe will come to you. When you believe there's a reason for everything and accept challenges and redirections in a loving way, knowing that further growth is imminent and around the corner from this discomfort, you will overcome challenge and end up stronger and more evolved than before.

Take time to examine your dominant thoughts and the life you have created. Journal or log the dominant thoughts that no longer serve you and bring you joy. Think of a word and color that represents each dominant thought that no longer serves your highest good. When the list is complete, across from each word and color, write a new word and color that represents the new thoughts or way of thinking that you will use as a replacement. Perhaps some of these new words will create your affirmations. Your affirmations may include: I am love; I attract love; I attract happiness; I attract joy; I attract healthy choices; I am abundance.

*

Sit quietly, in a comfortable position, close your eyes, breathe and begin to relax. Feel your body going deeper and deeper into relaxation. Breathe the breath of life, the gift that allows us to be human and be filled with love and life. Breathe and relax, letting all the anxieties, worries and burdens melt away. Allow every muscle in your body to relax. Begin with your feet and move up to the top of your head, loving and relaxing every muscle in your body.

Begin to visualize yourself as a magnet of love and abundance. See the light of love and abundance all around you. Feel the worthiness to behold all the gifts the Universe has to offer. Bring an abundance of love for yourself into your heart. Allow the love to swell your heart and picture the love saturating every cell of your heart until it spills over, like a cup runneth over. Allow the love to permeate every cell in your body. Allow your body to become love. Take pause to feel what that love feels like. Pay attention to how the cells in your body are reacting to this love. Feel the love saturate your being such that you feel like you're bursting with the emotion of love. Feel the love in your body and continue to breathe, breathe, breathe. If your mind wanders, bring your attention back to the breath and the feeling of love that permeates every cell in your body.

As a magnet of love, visualize love coming to you in all directions. Continue to visualize yourself drawing love from all directions. Feel that love of self and allow the joy from receiving love to cement itself into the crevices of your mind, body and spirit. As a magnet of abundance, visualize abundance, in whatever fashion you wish, coming to you in all directions. Continue to visualize yourself acquiring abundance from all sources. Focus on the energy of receiving. You are worthy to receive love and abundance.

In closing, allow yourself to be surrounded by an egg shaped white light with flecks of gold and silver, shimmering with love. Allow this light to envelop your body and extend into your energy fields about 3 feet away from you. Breathe in the light and just sit and relax, bathed in this love, and when your mind wanders, just bring it back to your breath and the light. When you feel complete, begin to feel the physical body and bring yourself back to your physical environment. Open your eyes and see a world that is brightened by the love you exude from your heart.

Resiliency

Resiliency is the ability to persevere and adapt to life when things don't go the way we had hoped or planned. Resiliency is the ability to handle the curve balls that life pitches to us. When we believe that there's a reason for everything and we maintain a calmness amidst the storm of defeat, we can overcome every obstacle placed in our path. We don't receive any challenges that are too great for us to handle. In our co-created plans, we placed boulders of challenge in our life's journey to demonstrate and prove our capabilities, strength, perseverance and resiliency to ourselves. In our creation, we also have been given every tool and resource we need to jump the hurdles, successfully. The fundamental obstacle in tapping into our inner strength and resiliency is in our thinking pattern. If we believe we will be overwhelmed with no hope in sight, that's exactly what we'll create—we'll be overwhelmed with no hope in sight. If we believe we have the tools and fortitude to overcome and steer through, we will.

Sometimes it's easier to take a challenge and break it down into smaller pieces. It's easier to get our arms around a breadbox than it is to get them around a refrigerator. When we recognize that there are no failures in life, just redirections, we can make it through and out, with love for ourselves and others, acknowledging that everything that happens is really in our highest good. It's not always easy to be grateful for the challenges, but it is a way to stay in a divine loop of love. Affirmations may include: I am resilient; I am strong; I am able to prioritize and handle stressful situations; I am a survivor.

*

Sit quietly, in a comfortable position, close your eyes and breathe and begin to relax. Feel your body going deeper and deeper into relaxation. Breathe in the breath of divine light and feel the light penetrate your body. Feel the white light around you, filling your lungs and bringing the healing vibration of perfection to all cells of the body. Breathe and relax, releasing all the anxieties, frustrations and stresses of the day. Begin at your feet and focus on every area, allowing each muscle in your body to release tension and relax. Continue to relax and become conscious of your breathing if your mind wanders.

Celebrate the times in your life when you've made wise choices and have shown great strength and fortitude when immersed in a challenge. Feel great love for the self, smile and allow the love and pride to flow throughout your body. Recognize that you are a stronger and more resilient person from the trials and tribulations that you've overcome in life. You can do anything. You can overcome any challenge. You have the tools to succeed within yourself. You are strong and resilient.

Allow yourself to see the light of the Universe pouring down from the heavens, entering your crown chakra, the bright star located about 6—8 inches above your head. Allow that light to form a white, glowing rod that envelops your spine. See the strength and power of that light as it illuminates the core of your being, the pillar that keeps your foundation strong and resilient. You may feel your shoulders rise and your spine begin to straighten. Know that you are aligned with the oneness in perfect harmony. Your higher self, your divine self is always present to make wise choices and support you during times of struggle. Congratulate yourself for this awareness.

Allow the light to sooth your body and penetrate every cell. Bath in this unconditional loving light and feel a level of healing and strength seldom recognized. Allow love to permeate all your cells and continue to breathe in the light, with confidence and knowing that you have the ability and wisdom to create the life you want. You deserve to be happy. You are worthy of happiness and inner peace.

Breathe in the light and just sit and relax, bathed in this love, and when your mind wanders, just bring it back to your breath and the light. When you feel complete, begin to feel the physical body and bring yourself back to your physical environment. Open your eyes and see a world that is brightened by the love you exude from your heart.

Re-Discover

Take time to re-discover your goodness and your talents and all the wonderful aspects of your life that you have created. Rekindle the love you have for the self and take great pride in all your achievements, both big and small. Skip the focus on the aspects of yourself that you think need to improve and focus on those parts that are loving, kind, grateful, compassionate, considerate, generous, tolerant, peaceful, flexible, and adaptable. If you focus on what is good, it will expand. Expand your belief in yourself. Allow the habits you hold dear to prosper and override any habit that you don't admire. When we focus on something, it comes into clearer view. When we concentrate on something it expands. When we think in some given manner and exude energy connected to that thought process, we attract that which we exude. You already know of your divine nature, you just need to remember it. Remember and re-discover. The beauty and perfection are within. Affirmations may include: I am that I am; I am love; I am light; I am.

*

Sit quietly, in a comfortable position, close your eyes, breathe and begin to relax. Feel your body going deeper and deeper into relaxation. Breathe the breath of life, the gift that allows us to be human and be filled with love and life. Breathe and relax, letting all the anxieties, worries and burdens melt away. Allow every muscle in your body to relax. Begin with your feet and move up to the top of your head, loving and relaxing every muscle in your body.

Begin to visualize yourself as a shimmering oval globe of white and gold light. Visualize rays of focused light emanating from your heart. Know that there is a wise and trusted part of yourself that is always divinely connected to unconditional love. Feel the worthiness to behold all the gifts the Universe has to offer. Bring an abundance of love for yourself into your heart. Allow the love to swell your heart and picture the love saturating every cell of your heart until it spills over, like a cup runneth over. Allow the love to permeate every cell in your body. Allow your body to become love. Take pause to feel what that love feels like. Pay attention to how the cells in your body are reacting to this love. Feel the love saturate your being such that you feel like you're bursting with the emotion of love. Feel the love in your body and continue to breathe, breathe, breathe. If your mind wanders, bring your attention back to the breath and the feeling of love that permeates every cell in your body.

When you are ready, allow yourself to be surrounded by an egg shaped white light with flecks of gold and silver, shimmering with love. Allow this light to envelop your body and extend into your energy fields about 3 feet away from you. Breathe in the light and just sit and relax, bathed in this love, and when your mind wanders, just bring it back to your breath and the light. When you feel complete, begin to feel the physical body and bring yourself back to your physical environment. Open your eyes and see a world that is brightened by the love you exude from your heart.

Joy

Joy! The joy we are discussing and meditating upon is *joy as a state of being, not as an emotion.* One day at a time, put love in your heart, joy in your step and vibrate to the tune of gratitude. Each day, our true essence continues to emerge when we put joy into every thought and every action. If by chance you cannot put joy into a situation, ask yourself, "Why?" You have two choices when you reach a place in your life where you cannot put joy into your thoughts, words, and actions. You can stop doing whatever it is—or you can surrender. In many instances we have made choices in life that we may regret or may no longer be serving our highest good. Sometimes, for many reasons, we just can't walk away. In that case, we must surrender to bring joy back into our life. In this surrender, we accept the circumstances until we can remove them from our life or they no longer exist. In a state of joy, love and gratitude reside. Life occurs with greater ease and more blissful existence results. If you want life to be joyous, be joy. Affirmations may include: I decide joy; I am joy; I live in a state of joy.

*

Sit quietly, in a comfortable position, close your eyes, breathe and begin to relax. Feel your body going deeper and deeper into relaxation. Breathe the breath of life, the gift that allows us to be human and be filled with love and life. Breathe and relax, letting all the anxieties, worries and burdens melt away. Allow every muscle in your body to relax. Begin with your feet and move up to the top of your head, loving and relaxing every muscle in your body. Take a few cleansing breaths (big inhalation and exhalation) and resume a normal breathing rhythm. Visualize yourself in your favorite place. This can be a place you have been, a place you have seen in pictures, or a place you imagine. Experience the joy in being. Feel the love you have for where you are. See yourself and feel a magnitude of love for yourself. Feel the connection to spirit. See the Angels that surround you and feel their love as they have guided your steps since birth. Feel joyful—become joy. Be joy. When you step into a state of joy, joy comes back to you. Commit yourself to a life of joy. Make a decision to put joy into every breath such that you become joy. Sit and feel a sense of joy. Recall people and aspects of life that bring you joy and remain in this state for as long as you wish.

When you are ready, allow yourself to be surrounded by an egg shaped white light with flecks of gold and silver, shimmering with love. Allow this light to envelop your body and extend into your energy fields about 3 feet away from you. Breathe in the light and just sit and relax, bathed in this love, and when your mind wanders, just bring it back to your breath and the light. When you feel complete, begin to feel the physical body and bring yourself back to your physical environment. Open your eyes and see a world that is brightened by the love you exude from your heart and feel the joy just to be alive.

Rain

Rain flows from the earth's watering can so that life can be sustained and new birth can be gifted. Rain can be a lovely metaphor for challenge and opportunity. As we grow from infancy, we all have some magnitude of rain that allows us to sprout and ripen. Whether we flourish and thrive or rot from that magnitude of rain, however, is the choice of each individual. We are not victims of our path in life. We have co-created our earthy journey to allow for the evolution of soul. The destination of the journey is to seek the peace and bliss that life is intended to offer through the realization of our co-created plans and our return to the oneness of our total existence. When we truly understand that we are one with everyone and everything, realignment occurs as it was in the beginning. In this realignment is a realization of our true self.

We can move forward in our evolution of self but we cannot change the past. When we accept, however, that regardless of how painful our past was, we were the co-authors of that plan, we begin to ask ourselves why? There is no blame but there is a reason. The specificity of the reasons may not be elucidated for many, many years but the important concept is that there was a reason and it's always an opportunity for growth. It is good to give thanks for the opportunities to evolve and expand our levels of consciousness. Affirmations may include: I am strong because of the challenges I have overcome; there is no challenge I cannot overcome; every challenge is an opportunity for my growth and will teach me and show me how strong I really am.

*

Sit quietly, in a comfortable position, close your eyes, breathe and begin to relax. Feel your body going deeper and deeper into relaxation. Breathe the breath of life, the gift that allows us to be human and filled with love and life. Breathe and relax, letting all the anxieties, worries and burdens melt away. Allow every muscle in your body to relax. Begin with your feet and move up to the top of your head, loving and relaxing every muscle in your body. Bring the white light of the Universe into your crown chakra and allow it to envelop you in love and light.

With this love and light in your heart, review the rain that has fallen on your life through the years. Give thanks for the rain, as you would not have grown to be who you are without it. Open your mind and your heart and let yourself imagine actual rain falling on you as a shower of love and allow it to cleanse and heal those wounds of the past that before now you have not appreciated. You may not understand them now, but if you have faith that you co-created your plan for your growth and evolution you can accept and appreciate their occurrence and move on. You can change your outlook and change your life. You can create your new existence with the support of a Universe and Divine Infrastructure that loves you. Remain in this state of love for as long as you wish.

When you are ready, allow yourself to be surrounded by an egg shaped white light with flecks of gold and silver, shimmering with love. Allow this light to envelop your body and extend into your energy fields about 3 feet away from you. Breathe in the light and just sit and relax, bathed in this love, and when your mind wanders, just bring it back to your breath and the light. When you feel complete, begin to feel the physical body and bring yourself back to your physical environment. Open your eyes and see a world that is brightened by the love you exude from your heart. Be the sunshine that can render your life and the earth dry from the rainiest of days.

Gratitude and Love

The world will be a better place, when gratitude and love are the primary emotions that fuel our existence. When challenges arise, look not at the face value but at the deep, divine reason for their existence. Trust yourself and give thanks for the opportunity to grow in love. Maintain feelings of gratitude for the beauty and abundance of the planet. When life isn't going quite the way you'd prefer, count your blessings instead of your burdens. Love is divine and our glimpse of heaven comes from the feelings of love that we give and receive every day. Affirmations may include: I am grateful; I am blessed; I am love; I am gratitude.

*

Sit quietly, in a comfortable position, close your eyes, breathe and begin to relax. Feel your body going deeper and deeper into relaxation. Breathe the breath of life, the gift that allows us to be human and filled with love and life. Breathe and relax, letting all the anxieties, worries and burdens melt.

Allow a slide show to begin in your mind. One slide after another continues to appear, all capturing the many blessings in your life and the gifts that mother earth provides to her children. Allow the gratitude you feel for all your blessings to permeate every cell in your body. Allow the gratitude you feel for the earth and all its gifts to fill your heart and permeate every cell in your body. Allow the love for the blessings to fill your heart and spill over, like a cup runneth over, permeating every cell in your body. Allow your body to become love and gratitude. Take pause to feel what that love and gratitude feels like. Pay attention to how the cells in your body are reacting to this love and gratitude. Feel the gratitude saturate your being such that you feel like you're bursting with the emotion of love and incredible thanks.

Sit and enjoy the feelings of love and gratitude and continue to breathe. If your mind wanders, bring your attention back to the breath and the feeling of love and gratitude that permeates every cell in your body. Picture our loving planet earth and send love and gratitude to it for all it gives each moment of the day. Send love from your heart to all people, especially those who do not know love or cannot give thanks.

When you are nearing completion, allow gratitude and love to linger and make a commitment to yourself to give thanks and count blessings throughout the day. The more often we feel love and gratitude, the more deeply this feeling becomes integrated into our being.

In closing, allow yourself to be surrounded by an egg shaped white light with flecks of gold and silver, shimmering with love. Allow this light to envelop your body and extend into your energy fields about 3 feet away from you. Breathe in the light and just sit and relax, bathed in this love and gratitude, and when your mind wanders, just bring it back to your breath and the light. When you feel complete, begin to feel the physical body and bring yourself back to your physical environment. Open your eyes and see a world that is brightened by the love you exude from your heart.

* * *

May the world be filled with peace, love and abundance because of the reflection you provide from the . . . .

Inside-Out

Suggestions

Books

Daniel J. Benor, MD—*Spiritual Healing—Scientific Validation of a Healing Revolution*
Deepak Chopra, MD—*Quantum Healing*
Jim Collins—*Good To Great*
Dr. Masaru Emoto—*The Hidden Messages in Water*
Richard Gerber, MD—*Vibrational Medicine*
Valerie Hunt, PhD—*Infinite Mind*
Bruce Lipton, PhD—*The Biology of Belief*
Carolyn Myss, PhD—*Anatomy of a Spirit*
James L. Oschman, PhD—*Energy Medicine, the Scientific Basis*
Candice Pert, PhD—*Molecules of Emotion*
Karen Reivich and Andrew Shatte—*The Resilience Factor: 7 Keys to Finding Your Inner Strength and Overcoming Life's Hurdles*
Lt. Col. Rob "Waldo" Waldman—*Never Fly Solo*
Robert M. Williams—*PSYCH-K...The Missing Peace In Your Life!*
Diane Zimberoff—*Breaking Free From the Victim Trap: Reclaiming Your Personal Power*
Gary Zukav—*The Dancing WuLi Masters*

The Movie

What the Bleep Do We Know

The Program

Becoming The Totally Responsible Person (TRP) © *: Enhancing Personal Success*
TRP Enterprises, Inc. www.trpnet.com   trperson@aol.com

CPSIA information can be obtained at www.ICGtesting.com
Printed in the USA
BVOW06s0221130916

461958BV00026B/214/P